TO JERRY, MY CAMERAGUY

Your never-ending support and belief in me made this book possible. Because of your creativity behind the camera, we made that first garden video that changed our lives. Together, we are an incredible team.

AND TO MY MOM AND DAD, MY FIRST GARDEN TEACHERS

Your love for me and for each other has shaped my life beyond words.

CONTENTS

Introduction Turning Your Dream to Reality—No Experience Required . . . 8

1 Why I Grow My Own Food and Why You Should (and CAN) Too . . . 10

2 Start Simple and Expand Later . . . 18

3 The Secret to Gardening on a Budget—Starting Seeds Indoors . . . 28

4 Transplanting and Transitioning Indoor Seedlings to the Great Outdoors . . . 54

5 Placement of Your Garden and How to Prep It for Planting . . . 64

6 Watering—The Key to a Productive Garden . . . 78

7 Planting Vegetable Seedlings in the Garden . . . 90

8 Garden Challenges—Pest and Disease Control, Extreme Weather . . . 116

9 Harvesting Organic Vegetables Like a Pro . . . 126

10 Revel in the Rewards—The Garden Gives Back . . . 144

Appendix 1 CaliKim's Quick Look—Warm-Weather Veggies . . . 149

Appendix 2 CaliKim's Quick Look—Cool-Weather Veggies . . . 151

Glossary Basic Gardening Terms Explained . . . 152

Resources . . . 154

About the Author . . . 156

Index . . . 157

INTRODUCTION

Turning Your Dream into Reality—
No Experience Required

IMAGINE STEPPING OUTSIDE on a sunny afternoon with a basket in your hands, a cool breeze blowing, birds chirping, and butterflies flitting around. Everything is colorful, blossoming, and lush. You stroll through your beautiful garden filled with crimson-red tomatoes, multicolored peppers, leafy lettuce, bright kelly green cucumbers, and squash the size of baseball bats. You take a deep breath—the heady fragrance of mint and lavender fills your senses. You pause for a moment to take it all in, then eagerly begin.

What are you doing? Picking dinner—right from your own backyard. You fill your basket to the brim with succulent, colorful vegetables and flavorful herbs. You bring your basket, overflowing with freshness and flavor, to your kitchen and you prepare a delectable,

fresh-from-the-garden meal for your family. You feel proud knowing you are providing your loved ones with healthy, organic food that you grew yourself. You know exactly where it came from and what is in it.

Sound like a dream that's completely out of reach? Have you been reluctant to grow a garden because it seems complicated, expensive to get started, and time consuming? Do you want to grow wholesome, homegrown, organic vegetables, but don't know how?

I used to feel the same way before I started my own backyard garden. I was tired of eating tasteless vegetables from the grocery store. I was concerned about the effects the pesticides and other chemicals sprayed on store-bought produce might have on my family's health. I wanted a

backyard garden grocery store of my own with organic, flavorful vegetables. However, I wasn't sure how to get started, and I didn't think I could fit gardening into my busy life as a wife and mom of two young kids.

If you can relate, then it's time for you to take matters into your own hands and start growing your own organic vegetables. Even if you have never grown anything before, have no idea where to start, and have no space for a garden, you can grow your own organic vegetables that are fresh and full of flavor—just like I did.

Organic Gardening for Everyone is for people just like YOU. It's a hands-on guide to growing your own organic vegetables—from seed to harvest— in a simple and inexpensive way that fits into your lifestyle. I share with you how to get your garden started, care for it, and harvest it, step by step, with lots of color photographs, making it easy for you to know exactly what to do.

And you know what the best part is? You're not alone. We're doing this together. I'll be with you every step of the way. Take this book out in the garden with you. Learn how to grow organic veggies with your kids, significant other, or a friend. Get everyone involved. You can grow a garden—with no previous experience, and no matter how little space you have.

Before you know it, you'll be growing your own food and sharing it with those you love, and you'll have tons of fun doing it.

TURN YOUR DREAM INTO REALITY

I can't wait for your dream of growing your own organic vegetables to become a reality for you. Soon **you'll** be the one stepping outside on a sunny afternoon with a basket in your hand. What are you doing? Harvesting dinner—the first vegetables you grew in your own backyard.

You'll experience an incredible feeling of accomplishment as you bring that basket, brimming with freshness and flavor, in your kitchen. And you'll be proud to prepare a garden-fresh meal of nourishing, delicious food for your family.

It's time to discover the magic of planting a seed and watching it grow into the most amazing vegetables you've ever eaten. It's addicting. And I guarantee you'll never go back.

1

WHY I GROW MY OWN FOOD AND WHY YOU SHOULD (AND CAN) TOO

I GREW UP IN COLORADO, the third of ten kids. With so many mouths to feed, my parents grew a large garden to save money on groceries. The entire family spent many hours working together in the garden, picking endless rows of beans, husking corn, and harvesting tomatoes, lots of zucchini, and many other vegetables.

We ate tasty meals from our own garden almost daily, and all the kids helped my mom preserve the vegetables that we grew. Our freezer was stuffed with beans, corn, and peppers. Our basement shelves were lined with colorful rows of canning jars filled with pickles, salsa, beets, zucchini relish, and homemade ketchup. It was too cold to grow anything outdoors in the winter, so it was a huge treat to eat food we harvested and preserved the summer before.

To be honest, as child, gardening wasn't love at first sight. At times the garden tasks seemed endless.

A FAMILY THAT GARDENS TOGETHER STAYS TOGETHER

Looking back now, I can see that my parents created a sense of family fun, teamwork, and togetherness in the garden. Although I didn't realize it at the time, being raised with a vegetable garden created an appreciation within me for garden-fresh fruits and vegetables. It also gave me the desire as an adult to grow my own food and create those memories for my own family.

After I married my husband, Jerry, we moved to Southern California and had our two children, Julianne and Drew. For several years, we lived in small condos or apartments with no space to garden (or so I thought). I became increasingly concerned about the effect processed food, pesticides, and chemicals sprayed on grocery store fruits and vegetables can have on our bodies. I worried about the possible adverse long-term effects this may have on our children. And I was tired of tasteless store-bought produce.

I remembered the incredible flavor of the homegrown vegetables I had as a child. I wanted to feed my family delicious, organic veggies, and I wanted to have the satisfaction of growing them myself. I dreamed of a beautiful garden filled with vegetables, herbs, and flowers, where I could get my hands dirty, grow my own healthy food, and build my own happy family memories, just as I did growing up.

MY PROBLEMS

But I didn't know where to start. You see, there were several problems—and I didn't think my dream would ever be a reality.

Problem 1: I was a busy wife and the mom of two young kids. I didn't think I had the extra hours in my day to maintain a garden.

Problem 2: We were a one-income family. I was a stay-at-home mom with little room in our tight budget for supplies.

Problem 3: It had been years since I gardened as a child, and I remembered very little about how to grow veggies. I began researching and was immediately overwhelmed by all the information and options. It all seemed so complicated, and I didn't know how to get started.

Problem 4: Our small condo didn't have a yard, and there was no space for a garden. With the high price of California housing, I didn't think we would ever be able to purchase a house with a backyard.

IT ALL STARTS WITH DESIRE

Eventually, we were finally able to purchase our own home with a backyard. Our house sat on an unusable weed-filled hill, with a grassy flat space at the bottom. There was no question in my mind that I would grow veggies. It was the garden space I had long dreamed of.

That first year, I knew nothing about starting seeds indoors. I didn't know about easy, inexpensive gardening methods. I didn't have a clue about how to garden organically. What I did have was a huge desire and a dream to have my own garden. More than anything, I wanted to get my hands in the soil, grow my own food, and feed my family healthy vegetables. I was determined, and I dove in headfirst.

I borrowed a rototiller from a friend and went to work carving out my new garden space in a corner of the yard. The next weekend was Mother's Day. My only request was for the entire family to spend the day planting our garden. My kids complained—just like I did at their age when gardening with my parents—but it didn't bother me. I was happy that we were outside together, digging in the dirt, planting vegetables, and building memories. At the end of the day, I was content knowing that we had spent time together as family and our own fresh veggies would be on our dinner plates soon.

This photo shows what our backyard looked like when we first moved in. As you can see, there wasn't much there when we started. To see how different it looks now, take a look at page 15.

First Harvest: I Was Hooked

A few months later, I harvested my very own fresh-from-the-garden lettuce, tomatoes, and cucumbers. I'll never forget that day. The taste of the fresh vegetables was out of this world, and I had an incredible feeling of pride knowing I was feeding my family a tasty meal that I grew myself.

From that moment on, I was hooked. And I haven't stopped growing since. This passion was the stepping-stone to teaching others how to grow their own food.

THE BIRTH OF THE
CALIKIM GARDEN & HOME
YOUTUBE CHANNEL

The following year, we were chosen to be on a backyard makeover TV show. It was an incredible experience, and it allowed us the opportunity to landscape our yard and terrace our weedy hill. This gave us the space to expand our vegetable garden, and I busily got to work planting.

My husband Jerry's (aka "CameraGuy") passion is video and photography. On a challenge with a few of his camera buddies to make a viral video, he shot a video of me explaining how to fertilize my vegetables with compost in my newly

expanded garden. On a whim, we posted it on YouTube. To our surprise, people started watching, subscribing, and asking for more.

I still felt like a newbie with much to learn. I asked viewers for tips and advice, and I incorporated their suggestions into my gardening videos. We made more videos on starting seeds indoors and transplanting seedlings in the garden. As I learned, my garden and our channel grew by leaps and bounds. We posted more tutorial videos focusing on quick, simple, inexpensive, organic methods that made it doable for everyone to grow veggies, no matter how little experience or space they had.

While that first video didn't go viral, we realized that our individual skills were a powerful match. I love the thrill of seeing a new gardener discover the magic of seeing a seed sprout and grow, harvesting it, and taking the first bite of their own homegrown veggie. Jerry loves being creative behind the camera, capturing the unusual shots that make our videos unique and producing a video that is visually appealing.

As we communicated our excitement for growing and eating organic vegetables, our YouTube channel and community began to grow.

Viewers loved learning the basic skills they needed to be successful growing their own food.

This formula for instruction has proven itself—literally a million times over. People from all over the world are now watching our videos and learning to grow their own food. They're part of our garden community and having a lot of fun along the way. To watch garden tutorials on our YouTube channel, go to calikimgardenandhome.com/gardeningvideos.

WHY GROW YOUR OWN FOOD?

There's nothing quite like growing your own food. What hooked me in the beginning was the superior flavor, freshness, and variety of homegrown food. There is also the cost savings, and knowing I am eating produce that is organic, fresh, and not sprayed with pesticides. When you grow your own food, you have control over what goes in it. You know what amendments you put in the soil, what you fed the plants, and how you tended to the food you harvest and eat.

I also love the outdoors: the feeling of warm sun on my back and getting my hands in the soil. It's what I like to call garden therapy.

Flavor and Freshness

Have you ever had a tomato that tasted like cardboard or purchased a bag of slimy greens from the grocery store? Many fruits and veggies at the grocery store are picked half-ripe for storage and shipping, and they are often bland and tasteless. Homegrown fruits and vegetables have an intensity of flavor that goes above and beyond the flavor of store-bought produce.

Growing your own produce allows you to harvest it at the peak of ripeness. This is why vine-ripened homegrown tomatoes are so much more flavorful than store-bought tomatoes. Homegrown lettuce that is harvested at its peak brims with freshness, flavor, color, and texture.

There is nothing more delicious and nutritious than a garden-to-table meal—it just doesn't get any fresher. Once you experience the taste of homegrown veggies, you'll never go back.

Variety

Colorful, organic produce can be grown right in your own backyard. And you can grow an endless variety—much more than is available at the grocery store. Nearly any type of herb, flower, fruit, or vegetable can be grown in your garden, especially when you start your garden from seed. (This will depend on your climate and growing conditions, but—trust me—there will be plenty to choose from.)

Cost

Organic produce at the grocery store sells at a premium price. Instead of spending hundreds of dollars a month on organic, store-bought fruits and vegetables, why not spend a few dollars for seeds and soil and grow your own groceries for a fraction of the cost?

Grow what you like to eat and grow veggies that are expensive to purchase in the grocery store. You'll save a huge amount of money on groceries each month.

Organic Food

Many fruits and vegetables that are purchased at the store are sprayed with synthetic chemical fertilizers and pesticides. The long-term effects of these products are not fully known.

Growing organically is not difficult, and it doesn't have to be any more expensive than any other method. Organic gardening simply means you grow your veggies using compost, natural soils, organic fertilizers, and organic pesticides, and you avoid using synthetic chemicals in your garden.

When you put a plate of organic vegetables from your garden on the table, you know exactly where your food comes from. You'll have peace of mind knowing that you are protecting your family's health by eating organic, nutrient-dense food from your own backyard—and keeping the chemicals, pesticides, and preservatives off your table.

Garden Therapy

One of the most important reasons I love to grow my own food is that I find it therapeutic. The stress of the day melts away and I am rejuvenated in the garden. The fragrance of the fresh air, the vibrant greens of the plants, and the brilliant colors of the flowers, all make my senses come alive.

The feel of the soil in my hands, the warmth of the sun on my back, the thrill of seeing a seed grow, tending to the plants, and harvesting and eating the vegetables is all a very basic, simple pleasure. It's satisfying at the very core of my being. It's mentally refreshing and inspiring. It's pure magic.

WHAT ARE YOUR REASONS?

Knowing your reasons for wanting to grow your own food will give you inspiration and motivation. In addition to the reasons I've mentioned, maybe you have a serious food-related health issue and need to change your eating habits to regain your health. Or perhaps you want to teach your kids where food comes from in hopes that they will eat more fruits and vegetables. Or maybe you're like me—you love the joy of getting your hands dirty and the thrill of seeing the seeds pop through the soil.

No matter what your reason, you'll love growing your own food. Every time you put a plate of

garden-fresh organic vegetables on the table, it is worth the effort, because you'll know exactly what is in them and where they came from.

You may be saying, "Yes! I want to grow my own veggies—how do I start?" Even if you have absolutely no experience growing veggies—or you've tried to grow a garden before and haven't been able to—you *can* grow your own organic veggies. It's quick, simple, and inexpensive, and it's so much fun!

Let's begin together with my garden motto: Start simple and expand later.

2

START SIMPLE AND EXPAND LATER

> *"It's too complicated—I feel overwhelmed when I try to figure out how to start."*

> *"It takes too much time— I can't fit it into my busy schedule."*

> *"It's too expensive to buy the seeds and supplies. I can't afford it. It's cheaper to just buy veggies at the store."*

THIS IS WHAT SOME OF MY FRIENDS tell me when I ask why they don't grow their own organic vegetables. Sound familiar? Then you're in the right place.

Starting a garden can feel intimidating—but it doesn't have to. You don't need to plant an entire farm full of vegetables. You also don't need to have tons of spare time or have lots of space. You don't even need a huge budget to be a gardener. All you need is a dream, the desire, seeds, soil, and sunshine.

START SIMPLE: PLANT THE RIGHT VEGGIES IN THE RIGHT SEASON

I'm a firm believer that there is no such thing as a brown thumb. *Anyone* can grow their own food, no matter how much luck you've had growing veggies in the past or how little experience you have. With a few basic facts and a little bit of planning, you can easily grow fresh veggies many months out of the year (or year-round in warm climates).

Once you've settled on one or two vegetables that you enjoy eating, a key to starting simple is planting the right vegetables in the right season. Growing the right veggie at the right time of the year is the first step turning that brown thumb green. It puts you on the road to success in growing your own organic vegetables.

Working with the temperature range your favorite veggie grows best in is one of the secrets to easy gardening.

Dennis's dream was to grow his own fresh salads. One hot summer day, he headed outside to plant his first batch of lettuce seeds. He picked out a sunny spot in the garden, and he carefully loosened the soil. He sprinkled his seeds in the garden bed, gently covered them up with a handful of soil, and carefully watered them. He couldn't wait to see them sprout and checked on them daily. He waited. And waited. And waited some more. Nothing. He emailed me out of frustration: "What did I do wrong? The seeds never came up! I must have a brown thumb."

Dennis was missing a basic—but important—garden fact that would have made growing his much-anticipated salads a breeze and saved him a ton of frustration: Lettuce grows best in cool-weather and won't sprout in hot temperatures. Armed with this information, he tweaked his garden space and planted the seeds in part-shade to help them stay cooler. He was thrilled to see lettuce seedlings break through the soil in a few days. He also planted beans (a warm-weather vegetable) in the sunny spot. He

My garden motto is "start simple and expand later." Just get started—even if you only grow one thing and have just five minutes to spare.

Begin by asking yourself, "What vegetables do I like to eat?" Grow just one of them in a small container on a sunny windowsill.

Remember my garden motto: Start simple and expand later. Get started with one vegetable. Savor and taste the sweetness of garden success. Start with a dream, and with a little bit of effort, seeds, soil, and sunshine, you'll be shopping from your own organic grocery store before you know it.

FROM "I HAVE NO CLUE" TO "I'M GROWING VEGGIES!"

Angelica wanted to grow her own vegetables. She's a busy mom with two young children, and she hesitated because she had no clue what to do and didn't think she had time to start a garden. What she needed was something simple and doable. Angelica also wanted to teach her children where food comes from and hoped that it would encourage them to eat more fruits and vegetables.

I encouraged her to plant a small container of lettuce on her kitchen windowsill and include her children in the process. Once she'd grown lettuce in her kitchen window, I knew it would be easy for her to move to the next step, tucking seeds in the ground in a tiny patch of soil or planting an outdoor garden bed full of greens.

Angelica went for it. The whole family took a trip to the garden center to choose a container, a packet of lettuce seeds, and soil. Together, they filled the container with soil, planted the lettuce seeds, watered them, and placed their new mini garden in their sunny kitchen window. They lovingly cared for their little garden, and six weeks later they harvested their own delectable, fresh, organic greens and made their first garden-to-table salad.

Angelica was hooked and wanted to grow more. She expanded her kitchen windowsill lettuce garden by heading outdoors. She dug out a corner in her backyard, planted more lettuce—along with peppers, tomatoes, cucumbers, squash, and herbs—and she got the whole family involved in the process. Soon she was harvesting vegetables and making more garden-fresh meals. Her kids started asking for "all fruit" dinners and took small nibbles of the homegrown vegetables. She was proud of the food they were growing in their small backyard, and she loved every minute spent together in the garden as a family.

was thrilled to harvest fresh green beans about 6 weeks later.

There are two types of vegetables, cool-weather vegetables and warm-weather vegetables. Each type will grow and thrive—if it is planted at the right time of the year.

COOL-WEATHER VEGETABLES

You'll love growing cool-weather veggies, such as asparagus, beets, broccoli, brussels sprouts, cabbage, carrots, cauliflower, celery, chard, collards, kale, kohlrabi, lettuce, onions, peas, radishes, spinach, turnips, and all kinds of greens. Just think of all the garden-fresh meals you can make from these veggies—from a simple salad or a stir-fry packed with superfood greens, to kale smoothies, oven-roasted root veggies, and broccoli-cauliflower bakes. Is your mouth watering yet?

Now, I know you're dying to grow them ALL, but resist the urge to plant everything at once. Don't forget my garden motto: Start simple and expand later. Believe me, you'll thank me later. Pick just one or two of your favorites to start with so you don't get overwhelmed. Then, as your confidence grows, plant a few more each growing season. Even growing one or two vegetables means you'll be eating more homegrown goodness from your own backyard.

The Basics

These cool-season treats grow best in daytime temperatures between 40°F (5°C) and 75°F (23°C). Many cool-weather veggies will even tolerate light frosts (32°F/0°C), especially if the plants are well established when frost hits. When the temperatures hit 80°F (26°C) or higher, you may feel like jumping for joy (especially after a long, cold winter), but cool-weather veggies won't like it. The seeds won't germinate (sprout) in the heat, they won't grow if already germinated, and they definitely will not produce those delicious veggies you're craving.

For example, lettuce tends to turn bitter and shoot up a tall stalk from the center of the plant in high temperatures—a process referred to as bolting. Flowers grow from this center stalk, and when the flowers dry, seeds can be harvested. This is nature's way of producing the next generation of plants, but it's not a great way to grow a salad.

Secret to Success

Make it easy on yourself: Work with the best combination of vegetables and the weather, not against it. The secret to growing cool-weather veggies all the way to harvest is to plant them so that they mature when the weather is cool. The best time to plant them outdoors is a few weeks before the last frost date in the early spring so that they mature before the hot summer hits, or after the summer heat is gone, in the cooler days of fall. In a temperate winter climate, such as where I live in Southern California, the best time to grow cool-weather veggies is in the winter, when the weather is consistently under 75°F (23°C). They'll reward your tender loving care by producing lots of delicious, nutritious veggies to snack on right in the garden—or bring them inside and make a meal for your family.

Many cool-weather veggies can be direct seeded in the garden. Or start them from seed indoors when the temperature is too cold in the

late winter (for planting outdoors in early spring), or when it is still too hot in late summer (for planting outdoors in the fall). This way, you have seedlings to transplant outdoors when the temperature is right for them to thrive, saving you time and giving you the best chance of success in getting a harvest before the weather gets too hot.

You'll find all the details on starting seeds indoors in Chapter 3. For my video tutorial on how to start seed indoors, please visit calikimgardenandhome.com/gardeningvideos.

WARM-WEATHER VEGETABLES

After you've enjoyed your first few early spring, cool-weather veggies and you have success under your belt, you'll eagerly await the long, sunny, hot days of summer. This is the time to grow the classic warm-weather-loving veggies, such as beans, corn, cucumbers, eggplant, peppers, tomatoes, and squash.

Start your summer garden simple, with just one or two of your favorite warm-season veggies. Expand your garden to one or two more the next time you plant. One of the most popular warm-weather garden goodies you'll want to grow is tomatoes. I can't wait for you to taste your first homegrown tomato. The flavor is indescribable—far superior to the cardboard-tasting grocery store tomatoes. Once you taste your own, you'll never go back to store-bought tomatoes again.

The Basics

Warm-weather veggies can be planted outdoors once the last frost date in your area has passed. They thrive when they are planted in warm soil (at least 50–60°F/10–16°C), when the nighttime temperatures are between 60°F (15°C) and 75°F (23°C), and daytime temperatures are 75°F (23°C) to 90°F (32°C). Cool temperatures (less than 60°F/15°C) or overly hot temperatures (over 90°F/32°C) may slow their growth. Warm-weather veggies are cold sensitive, and frost will kill the plant in most cases.

Secret to Success

Make it easy on yourself: Plant warm-weather veggies so that they mature when the weather is warm. The secret to success is to plant them outdoors a few weeks after the last frost date of

the spring, as soon as the soil is warm. This gets them growing so they have as many of the warm summer days as possible to produce as many harvests as the weather allows. Late summer is also a good time to plant quick-maturing warm-weather crops, such as beans, squash, cucumbers, or my favorite dwarf tomato, Tiny Tim. As long as there is enough time for these frost-sensitive veggies to mature before the nights get colder, the days get shorter, and the frost hits, you are good to go.

First and Last Frost Date

If you're starting your garden with no previous experience, you may have heard a lot of talk about the first and last frost date. And you may have no idea what that means. Keep things simple: Use these dates to plan what veggies to plant and when to plant them. They are the most critical dates to know when starting a garden.

The "first frost date" is the average date of the first frost in the fall for the area in which you live. The "last frost date" is the average date of the last frost in the spring for the area in which you live. This is not an exact date but an estimation to help you know when to plant outside with only a small risk that your plants may be killed by frost. As a gardener, you always want to keep an eye on the weather forecast, plant accordingly, and use a winter cover, if necessary, over frost-sensitive plants.

For example, tomato plants are killed by frost, and you would not want to plant a tomato in the garden 30 days before your first frost date in the fall or 30 days before your last frost date in the spring. A tomato takes 60 to 90 days from the time it is planted outside until it is ready to

harvest. In either situation, it would be killed off by frost before it reached maturity.

If you are planting a cool-weather vegetable that is tolerant of frost, such as peas or kale, you can plant them outside as early as 2 to 3 weeks before your last frost date in the spring so that you are able to harvest as much as possible before the warm summer weather arrives. If they are planted in the fall, you would count backward from your first frost date so that your peas are ready or nearly ready to harvest before frost hits.

But how do you know what these critical dates are? Use an online U.S. and Canada frost date calculator, such as *The Old Farmer's Almanac*, bit.ly/FrostDateCalculator. Simply enter your zip code to see the dates for your location. In other parts of the world, seek out a regional frost date calculator to determine these dates or contact a local agricultural research facility or university. Note these dates on your calendar, and you'll be well on your way to growing a successful vegetable garden.

THE MAGIC OF GARDENING

When I first started my garden, I wasn't confident in my skills and didn't think of myself as a gardener. I wondered if I had the time or the money to grow veggies. Growing my own food seemed complicated, and I doubted whether I could do it.

Despite this, every time I grew a vegetable, harvested it, and ate it, I was thrilled! I learned a few tips and tricks along the way and my confidence grew. I expanded my garden and planted two or three more vegetables. I followed my curiosity and experimented with plants I had never grown before. I discovered the joy of being outdoors, digging in the dirt, and feeling the warm sun on my back. I found my passion and learned that there is more—much, much more—to gardening than just growing veggies. I felt alive in the garden, like I was creating something special. This is the magic of gardening.

You might feel overwhelmed and think growing vegetables is too hard, takes too much time, and is too pricey. Here's what I'd like to say to you: Every time you put fresh, organic vegetables on the table, it is worth the effort. The flavor is out of this world and you know exactly what they are grown with. You'll feel a one-of-a-kind satisfaction.

Start simple, expand later. Soon you'll be growing your own amazingly flavorful vegetables, be healthier as a result, and have a lot of fun along the way. And you'll discover the magic of gardening too.

You've got this. You're a gardener now.

Are you ready to dig in? Let's start some seeds indoors, the secret to gardening a budget.

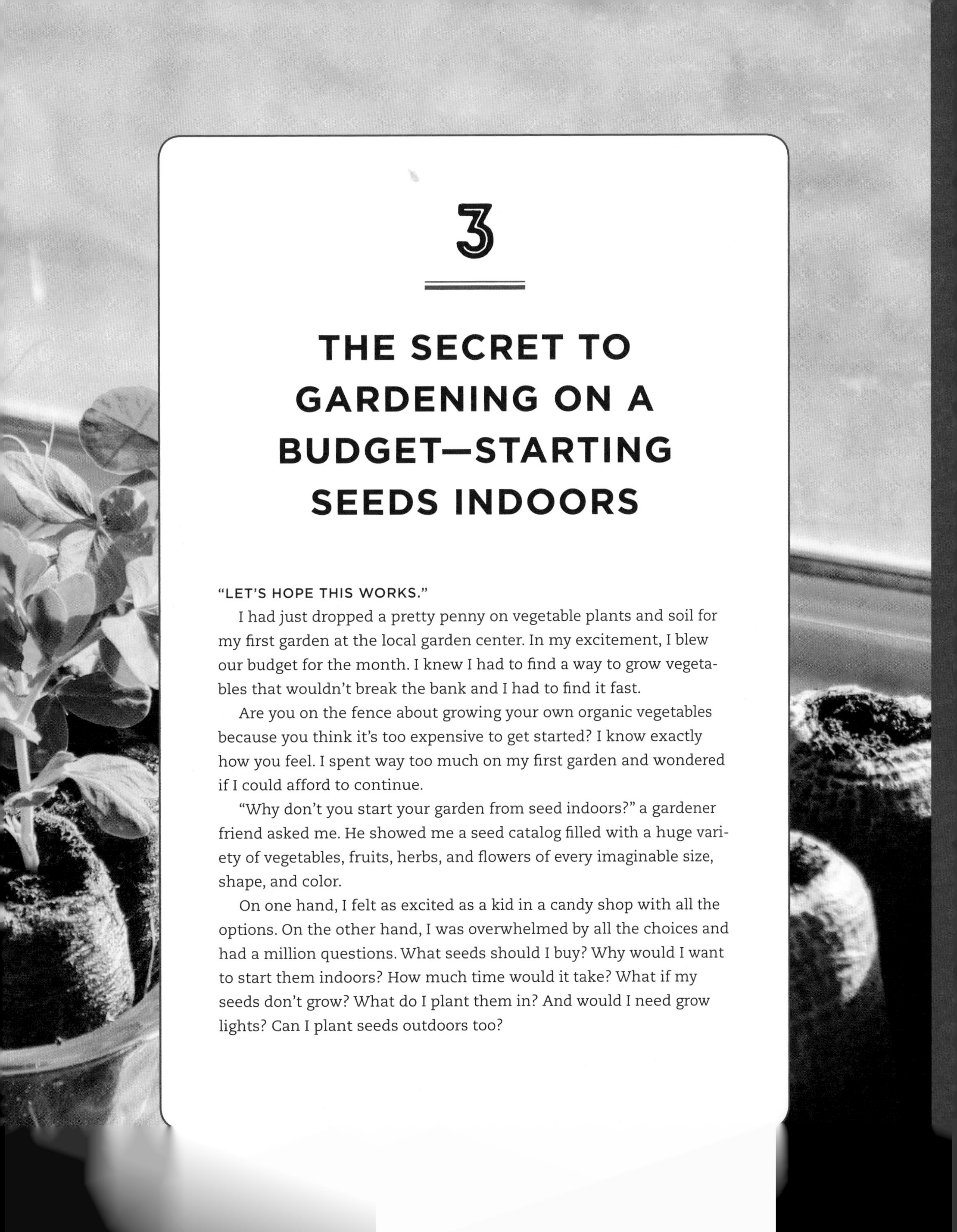

3

THE SECRET TO GARDENING ON A BUDGET—STARTING SEEDS INDOORS

"LET'S HOPE THIS WORKS."

I had just dropped a pretty penny on vegetable plants and soil for my first garden at the local garden center. In my excitement, I blew our budget for the month. I knew I had to find a way to grow vegetables that wouldn't break the bank and I had to find it fast.

Are you on the fence about growing your own organic vegetables because you think it's too expensive to get started? I know exactly how you feel. I spent way too much on my first garden and wondered if I could afford to continue.

"Why don't you start your garden from seed indoors?" a gardener friend asked me. He showed me a seed catalog filled with a huge variety of vegetables, fruits, herbs, and flowers of every imaginable size, shape, and color.

On one hand, I felt as excited as a kid in a candy shop with all the options. On the other hand, I was overwhelmed by all the choices and had a million questions. What seeds should I buy? Why would I want to start them indoors? How much time would it take? What if my seeds don't grow? What do I plant them in? And would I need grow lights? Can I plant seeds outdoors too?

Despite my uncertainty, I couldn't ignore the facts. When I compared the price of starting vegetables from seeds to the cost of purchasing vegetable plants, I was blown away. I could grow an entire farm full of tomatoes from one seed packet for less than the sticker price of a single tomato plant at the garden center. It was a no-brainer. Growing my garden from seed rather than purchased plants was the answer I was looking for.

Starting your garden from seeds isn't complicated. Once I learned how simple and inexpensive it is to start seeds, and what a blast it is to have eye-catching varieties and bright pops of color in the garden, growing vegetables from seeds was a game changer.

PENNIES ON THE DOLLAR

The next year, I planted my vegetable garden for pennies on the dollar compared to what I'd spent the year before. Because seed packets contain many seeds, the cost per plant is pennies (or less), compared to several dollars per plant at the garden center.

I soon learned I could put plate after plate of delicious organic vegetables on the table for our entire family and have plenty to share with friends, neighbors, and coworkers for a fraction of the cost.

VARIETIES THAT SIZZLE AND SPARKLE

Starting my garden from seed allowed me to venture far beyond the basic vegetable types available for purchase as transplants. It opened a whole new world of varieties, colors, shapes, and sizes, and it took my garden from ho-hum to sensational.

I discovered the delight of growing the rainbow—flaming orange tomatoes, purple peppers, and atomic red carrots. Ruffled bright green kale and frilly multicolored lettuces dazzled and danced their way through my garden. Giant eggplant and banana-shaped squash stole the show day after day.

Growing vegetables from seed allows me to create a glorious, relaxing outdoor space that dishes up mouthwatering vegetables, sizzles and sparkles with variety, has pizzazz, and reflects the colors I love.

GARDENING GOALS

"Always have something to harvest" is one of my gardening goals. Growing vegetables from seed gives me the option to plant something every few weeks and to plant vegetables that ripen at different times. This spreads out the harvest, so we always have something fresh and delicious from the garden to put on our table, but we're not overwhelmed with tons of vegetables all at once. Of course, living in the temperate growing environment of California makes this a possibility. But in colder climates, you can grow veggies year-round indoors or grow them under cover outside.

For example, one of my favorite tomatoes, Tiny Tim, is a dwarf plant that grows small 1-inch (2.5 cm) tomatoes in about 2 months. In contrast, the giant Yellow Brandywine tomato takes 3 to 4

months to mature. I plant both from seed at the same time, harvest the snackable Tiny Tims early in spring, and slice up Yellow Brandywines for sandwiches about a month later.

To further illustrate this, one of my favorite meals is a garden-fresh salad. I plant seeds for salad greens every few weeks, either indoors, outdoors, in containers, or in my raised beds. When one crop of greens has run its course, a fresh batch is ready to harvest. Growing from seed makes it simple and low cost to keep the harvests of delicious salad—and all kinds of other veggies—coming.

GET A HEAD START INDOORS

Rather than starting from seed **outdoors** when the weather is the right temperature, we're going to start seeds **indoors** to give you a head start on your garden. You'll grow your own strong, healthy transplants inside when it is too cold (or too hot) to grow them outside.

You'll then plant your homegrown transplants outside in the garden when the weather is the right temperature. This will save you time and money, and it will put fresh veggies on your dinner plate sooner.

Depending on the vegetable, you'll plant seeds inside 4 to 10 weeks before the last frost date in the spring (for warm-weather vegetables)

or before the first frost date in the fall (for cool-weather vegetables).

The seedlings will grow in your protected indoor environment in a sunny window or under grow lights, and they will remain indoors for several weeks. When the outside temperature is right for them to grow and thrive, you'll transplant the seedlings outdoors in your garden.

All it takes is 10 to 15 minutes to start vegetable seeds indoors. It really is that quick and easy.

But first things first—you need seeds.

CHOOSING SEEDS

Don't say I didn't warn you. Seeds are addicting. Once you are bitten by the seed-shopping bug, you'll be poring for hours over seed catalogs and online seed shops. There are endless types of seeds you can purchase (organic, rare, heirloom) and seeds for vegetables of every size, shape, and color.

You'll want to grow every one of these gorgeous veggies in your garden, and you will be tempted to buy seeds for them all.

When you are starting from seed for the first time, start simple. Purchase seed packets for a few vegetables that you like to eat. This gives you a sense of how much space you have to grow seeds indoors and what you like to grow. It also keeps you from getting overwhelmed. Once you learn some skills and gain confidence, expand your seed selection and your garden to your heart's desire.

Timing is everything when it comes to seed starting. Choose seeds for cool-weather vegetables if you are planting in the cooler months of early spring or fall, and warm-weather vegetables if you are planting in the late spring or warm summer months.

Don't Panic If Seeds Aren't Organic

To grow with organic seeds or non-organic seeds, that is the question.

Organic seeds come from plants grown without the use of synthetic fertilizers and pesticides. Here in the United States, seeds sold as organic are required to have a USDA (United States Department of Agriculture) stamp of approval on the label. There are certifying agencies in other parts of the world too. Be on the lookout for organic certification if that's important to you.

While growing with organic seeds is certainly a fantastic option, you can grow an organic garden with or without organic seeds. Seeds are only the beginning of the process of growing an organic garden. I am an organic gardener because I use compost, natural soils, and organic fertilizers and pesticides, and I avoid using synthetic chemicals in my garden. When I put a plate of organic vegetables from my garden on the table, I know exactly where my food comes from and what it's grown with, and I have the confidence that it's healthy and chemical-free.

WHERE TO GET THE GOODS

Basic seed varieties, organic and non-organic, can be purchased from your local garden center, but you'll get a much wider variety when you purchase from seed catalogs or online stores. There are endless options that will make you drool with anticipation. However, the enormous choices of seeds to purchase can be overwhelming.

My seed shop, calikimgardenandhome.com /seeds, takes the guesswork out of shopping for seeds and makes it easy for you to choose what to grow in your garden. The seeds are organized into collections, and they are themed according to seasons and types of vegetables. I personally selected each variety in each collection to make it simple and fun to start your garden from seed.

Now it's time to get your hands dirty and start your seeds indoors with my favorite quick, simple, and inexpensive methods: peat pellets and small containers with soil.

PEAT PELLETS: NO MUSS, NO FUSS

Starting seeds indoors doesn't get any simpler than when you choose to use peat pellets. Peat pellets are compressed discs of dry peat wrapped in a thin mesh netting. They are inexpensive and readily available, and they are a super speedy, doable, and convenient way to start seeds indoors. Just add water, fluff up the pellets, and plant your seeds. Kids love watching the pellets expand like magic when you add water.

Advantages

Peat pellets are convenient, with lots of fun sprinkled in. They take up very little space, and the setup and cleanup is minimal. Starting seeds in peat pellets doesn't involve purchasing (or making your own) seed-starting mix or getting your house messed up with bags of potting soil.

Disadvantages

Peat pellets, although relatively inexpensive, cost more than starting seeds in small containers with soil.

Supplies Needed

• Seeds for your favorite vegetables

• Peat pellets. These come in various sizes, separately or in kits that include a cover and tray to hold the pellets. They are available at most garden centers and online. I prefer to use loose pellets over kits due to the cost savings, and I prefer the larger 3-inch (7.5 cm) pellets over the smaller sizes. Seedlings can stay in the 3-inch pellets for the duration of their indoor growing time without the need to transplant them before putting them out in the garden.

• 2- to 3-inch (5 to 7.5 cm)-deep tray. Recycled meat trays, foil pans, or glass casserole dishes work well.

• Pencil

• Water

How to Start Seeds in Peat Pellets

STEP 1

Put the desired number of peat pellets in the tray. One vegetable variety will grow in each pellet. Some seeds may not sprout, so plant extra pellets for each vegetable so you have backup seedlings.

Cover the pellets with warm water. Watch them soak up the water and expand. This is the fun part—kids *love* it. Add more water if necessary.

STEP 2

Once the pellets are dark brown (5 to 10 minutes), they've soaked up enough water. Pour off the excess.

Open the top of the netting with a pencil and then loosen the top of the soil with the pencil.

STEP 3

Drop two to three seeds in each pellet in case one doesn't sprout. Don't stress if you drop in a few extra seeds; the seedlings can be thinned as they grow. Use the pencil to cover the seeds lightly with soil from the pellet. Label and date your seeds with a plant tag so you don't forget what you planted.

STEP 4

Mist the top of the pellets lightly with water from a spray bottle. Put your pellet tray in a sunny windowsill or under a grow light. Seeds will germinate in 2 to 14 days, depending on the variety.

CONTAINERS WITH SOIL

The most affordable method to start seeds is with small containers and potting soil. Using upcycled containers and making your own potting mix cuts down the cost even more. Many garden centers give away used six-pack plastic seedling trays and 3 to 4-inch-tall (7.5 to 10 cm) plastic pots. Used yogurt cups, sour cream containers, plastic cups, produce clam shells, takeout containers, and egg cartons are just a few of the items that can be washed and repurposed for seed-starting containers. Get creative—use whatever you have around the house.

Advantages

This method is especially effective for larger seeds that grow quickly, such as cucumbers, watermelon, or squash. It's less expensive than starting seeds in peat pellets, especially when using upcycled containers. Depending on the size of the container used, plants can stay in them for the duration of their indoor seedling phase without the need to transplant them before putting them out in the garden.

Disadvantages

Although still relatively quick, there are more steps involved with this method. It takes more time and is messier, and it requires more indoor space than pellets.

Supplies Needed

- Seeds for your favorite vegetables

- Small containers of your choice

- Organic bagged potting soil or seed-starting mix. Do not use outdoor garden soil. It may bring in pests, and it is not lightweight enough for germinating seeds in containers. Potting soil or seed-starting mix should be light and fluffy so seeds germinate quickly. Organic potting mixes are readily available at garden centers. To save even more money, make your own seed-starting mix.

- Nail and hammer or drill

- 2- to 3-inch (5 to 7.5 cm)-deep holding tray for the containers. Recycled meat trays, foil pans, cookie sheets, or glass casserole dishes work well.

- Small plastic tub for mixing soil

- Small shovel

- Water

How to Start Seeds in Containers with Soil

STEP 1

Place the desired number of containers in the holding tray. One vegetable variety will grow in each container or in each cell of the six-pack trays. Some seeds may not sprout. Start with extra containers so you have backup seedlings.

If the containers don't have holes, use a nail or a drill to add three to five drainage holes in the bottom of each.

STEP 2

Moisten the potting soil in a small plastic tub. Add a small amount of water, then mix it into the soil with a small shovel or trowel. Continue adding water and mixing until the soil is moistened all the way through to the consistency of crumbly brownie mix. There should be no dry soil pockets. Moistening the soil before seeds are planted helps the soil retain water and keeps the seeds moist as they germinate.

STEP 3

Fill the containers to just below the rim with potting soil. Drop two to three seeds in each container in case one doesn't sprout. Don't stress if you drop a few extra seeds in; the seedlings can be thinned as they grow. Cover the seeds lightly with soil and tamp the soil down gently to remove air pockets. Label and date your seeds with a plant tag so you don't forget what you planted.

STEP 4

Mist each container with water from a spray bottle. Put your container tray in a sunny windowsill or under a grow light. Seeds will germinate in 2 to 14 days, depending on the vegetable variety you are growing.

For a video tutorial on starting seeds indoors, please calikimgardenandhome.com/gardeningvideos.

INDOOR GROW LIGHTS— WHAT THEY ARE AND FOUR EASY SETUPS

You've started your seedlings. Now what? Light— and not just any old light but strong, intense light—is one of the most important factors to consider when growing indoor seedlings. Many gardeners grow their indoor seedlings on a sunny windowsill. However, often a sunny windowsill (even a south-facing window) doesn't have the 6 to 8 hours of direct overhead light that is required for seedlings to grow strong and healthy. When seedlings don't get enough direct overhead light, they stretch to get closer to the light. This causes their stems to grow tall and thin, or what is referred to as "leggy." A leggy seedling is a weak plant. It may be stunted and not grow into a productive vegetable.

If you're going to take the time to start your vegetable seeds indoors, growing them under grow lights is the best way to make sure they are stocky, healthy seedlings with strong stems. Strong seedlings will be able to withstand pests, wind, and the elements when the time comes to transplant them outdoors, and they'll produce lots of yummy veggies for you and your family to eat.

If you think setting up indoor grow lights sounds intimidating, you're not alone. I felt the same way the first time I started seeds indoors. Don't worry, this section takes the mystery out of it and makes it quick and simple so you know exactly what to do. You're about to learn about four easy grow light systems you can use to inexpensively provide grow lights for your indoor seedlings.

What Are Indoor Grow Lights?

Indoor grow lights are specifically designed for growing indoor seedlings. Instead of using an everyday lightbulb, you'll use a bulb with a specific intensity (lumens) and a specific type of light (kelvin) that mimics sunlight.

Lumens and Kelvin Explained

When shopping for bulbs, you will frequently see two specifications on the package: lumens and kelvin. It's important to have the right amount of lumens and the right kelvin to grow strong, healthy indoor seedlings. You might be confused about the difference between these terms, so let's break it down and make it easy to understand.

LUMENS

When you are growing vegetable seedlings indoors, it's critical that they are met with a very bright, intense light as soon as they germinate. Lumens is a measurement of brightness of light. Lumens are to light what pounds are

to tomatoes, or gallons are to milk. The higher the lumens the brighter the light, the lower the lumens the dimmer the light. Indoor vegetable seedlings need to be grown under a lightbulb that has between 1500 and 3000 lumens (the higher the better). This is so your plants don't get leggy and have the intense light they need to grow strong, stocky stems and healthy, green leaves.

KELVIN

Kelvin refers to the type of light produced or the color temperature of the lightbulb. Our goal is strong, green, healthy seedlings, and the grow lights we use need to mimic sunlight. Lightbulbs that are between 4500–6500 K (kelvin) are ideal for indoor seedlings. The higher the kelvin number, the closer the light is to daylight.

The number of lumens and kelvin a lightbulb has is specified on the package. There are many options available for both LED and CFL bulbs at hardware stores, as well as online. See Resources, page 154, for links to my favorite grow lights.

FOUR EASY GROW LIGHT SETUPS

Let's get your indoor grow lights set up with one of my four favorite quick, simple, and inexpensive methods: a clamp light, a grow light box, shop lights, or a simple tabletop grow light. Chose the setup that works best for you or a combination of all four, which is what I like to do.

SETUP 1: CLAMP LIGHT

The easiest and most inexpensive way to set up grow lights is with a simple clamp light with a cone-shaped metal reflector. The metal reflector concentrates the light to the area directly in front of it, so most of the light is directed toward your plants.

Advantages

A clamp light is super easy to set up and perfect for beginners as there is no assembly required. Just screw in the lightbulb, clip it overhead, and light up your seedlings. It's the most budget-friendly of the four setups I recommend, and the supplies are available at most hardware stores. A clamp light is easily attached to just about anything (e.g., shelves, cabinets, DIY clamp light station), making it ideal if you have a limited amount of space or are growing a small number of seedlings.

Disadvantages

A clamp light needs something to be clipped to, and it is only effective for one small tray or container of plants. If you'd like freestanding grow lights, or you want to grow a large number of seedlings, chose one of the other setups.

Supplies Needed

- Clamp light with an 8½- or 10-inch (21 or 26 cm) cone-shaped metal reflector

- CFL or LED screw-in lightbulb with the appropriate lumens and kelvin

- Clamp surface, such as a shelf or cabinet

- A shoe box or small pieces of wood to adjust the height of the seedling tray

(1)

How to Make a Clamp Light Setup

STEP 1

Screw the lightbulb into the clamp light fixture. Clamp the fixture onto a shelf or cabinet. Plug in the lamp and turn on the light.

STEP 2

Place your seedling tray directly underneath the light. To avoid leggy seedlings, the light should not be set up on an angle. It should be directly overhead, aiming straight down on the seedling tray. Raise up the seedling tray with a shoe box or small piece of wood so that it is no more than 1 to 2 inches (2.5 to 5 cm) from the light. As the plants germinate and grow taller, adjust the height of the tray so that the seedlings do not touch the light (this may scorch them). You want them to always be 1 to 2 inches (2.5 to 5 cm) away from the light; this prevents the seedlings from stretching for the light and becoming leggy.

STEP 3

Leave the lights on for 24 hours a day until the seedlings germinate so they are hit with intense light from the moment of germination. This helps avoid leggy seedlings. Once the seeds germinate, leave the lights on for 18 hours a day, off for 6 hours. Plug the light into a timer so it turns on and off automatically.

DIY CLAMP LIGHT STATION

If you don't have a shelf or cabinet to clip the light onto, making your own DIY clamp station is super simple and inexpensive.

SUPPLIES NEEDED

- 1-gallon (3.8 L) jug
- Sand
- 12-inch (30 cm) length of PVC pipe

STEP 1

Fill the jug halfway with sand. Place a 12-inch (30 cm) length of PVC pipe into the jug, through the sand to the bottom of the jug. Clip the light onto the PVC pipe.

STEP 2

Place the seedling tray directly underneath the clamp light, adjusting the height of the light as the seedlings grow so that it is always no more than 1 to 2 inches (2.5 to 5 cm) away from the seedlings.

SETUP 2: GROW LIGHT BOX

A grow light box is a simple, efficient way to use a clamp light to grow seedlings. Gary Pilarchik from The Rusted Garden YouTube Channel (www.youtube.com/user/pilarchik) is the originator of this method, and I've used it for several years with great success.

The grow light box uses a 30-gallon (114 L) plastic storage tub lined with aluminum foil (optional, to reflect the light on the plants). The lid has a hole cut in the top, and the clamp light is attached to the inside of the lid—positioned directly above the seedlings. Seedlings are placed in the box and grown there for 4 to 6 weeks, or until they are ready to be planted outside.

Advantages

A grow light box works well for a small number of plants. It's easy, inexpensive to make, and portable. It also keeps seedlings neat, tidy, contained in one place, and out of sight. The light is used in an enclosed space, and there is less light "waste" and more light directed toward the plants. In addition, the aluminum foil reflects the light, resulting in more light directed toward the plants for faster growth. Not only that, but because the plants are contained in the box, they stay warmer. This is ideal for growing warm-weather seedlings, such as tomatoes, cucumbers, squash, or peppers.

Disadvantages

At times the grow light box can get too warm for cool-weather seedlings. It can also build up humidity, causing mold to grow on the soil. Leave the lid ajar to provide airflow and to cool the inside of the box. Another disadvantage is that the space is limited. As a result, you can only grow a small number of seedlings. If you are growing lots of plants, make two grow light boxes—or use setup 3, the shop light setup.

Supplies Needed

- Sharp scissors or a box cutter

- 30-gallon (114 L) plastic storage tote with a lid, or larger to hold more plants

- Clamp light fixture and lightbulb

How to Make a Grow Light Box

STEP 1

Using scissors or a box cutter, cut a hole in the center of the lid for the clamp light. The hole should be about 6 inches (15 cm) square. Cut a slit from one end of the hole toward the edge of the lid for the light to be clipped to. If you have a large bin, a hole and slit can be made on each end of the lid so that two clamp lights can be attached to the lid for even light coverage.

STEP 2

Position the clamp light under the lid. Squeeze the clamp handle, poking one side of the clamp through the hole and clamping onto the slit in the lid.

STEP 3

Place the seed tray in the grow light box, then place the lid on the box. Seedlings should always be no more than 2 inches (5 cm) away from the light to avoid leggy seedlings. Place a shoe box or brick underneath the seedling tray to raise it up to the proper level. Adjust the height as the plants grow. Leave the lid ajar to reduce the humidity and avoid mold on the soil. Leave the light on for 24 hours a day until seedlings germinate so they are hit with intense light from the moment of germination. This helps avoid leggy seedlings. Once they germinate, leave the lights on for 18 hours a day, off for 6 hours. Plug the light into a timer so it will turn on and off automatically.

SETUP 3: SHOP LIGHT SETUP

Setting up grow lights with a 4-foot (1.2 m) shop light is simple and versatile. It can be attached to shelves or made into a portable setup.

Advantages

This setup is ideal for larger numbers of seedlings. It is also a quick and easy setup to make.

Disadvantages

Although less inexpensive than ready-made grow lights, a shop light setup costs more than a clamp light or grow light box. Consider your available indoor growing space, as shop lights have a larger footprint than the other recommended setups.

Supplies Needed

- 2- or 4-foot (61 cm or 1.2 m) shop light fixture

- Compact fluorescent or LED bulbs to fit the size of your shop light fixture

- Two 6-inch (15 cm) chains and 4 S hooks, usually included with the shop light fixture

- Two cup hooks, if you are attaching to a wooden shelf

- A shoebox or blocks of wood to adjust the height of the seedling trays

How to Make a Shop Light Setup

STEP 1

After inserting the bulbs into the shop light fixture, suspend the light from a shelf so it shines down on the plants. For wooden shelves, screw a cup hook into the underside in the middle at each end of the shelf. Suspend the shop light from the cup hooks, using the chain and hooks provided with the light fixture. Attach a hook to the opposite end of each chain and use the hook to hang the light from the cup hook.

For a wire shelf, attach the S hook and chain directly to an upper shelf so the light is suspended from that shelf and shines down on the seedlings on the shelf below.

STEP 2

Place the seedling tray under the shop light 1 to 2 inches (2.5 to 5 cm) away from the light. Use shoe boxes or blocks of wood to raise up the seedling trays close to the light. As the plants grow, adjust the height of the trays by removing boxes or blocks of wood so plants do not touch the light. Adjust the length of the chain to move the light higher or lower as needed. The seedlings should always be no more than 1 to 2 inches (2.5 to 5 cm) from the light.

STEP 3

Leave the light on for 24 hours a day until seedlings germinate so they are hit with intense light from the moment of germination. This helps avoid leggy seedlings. Once the seeds germinate, leave the lights on for 18 hours a day, off for 6 hours. Plug the light into a timer so it turns on and off automatically.

PORTABLE DIY SHOP LIGHT STATION

If you do not have shelves, it's easy and inexpensive to make your own DIY shop light station.

SUPPLIES NEEDED

- Two 1-gallon (3.8 L) jugs
- Two 12-inch (30 cm) lengths of PVC pipe
- Sand, enough to fill the gallon containers halfway full
- Three to four shoe boxes and/or various blocks of wood

STEP 1

Fill both jugs halfway with sand. Insert a 12-inch (30 cm) length of PVC pipe into each jug, passing it through the sand to the bottom of the jug. This will keep your shop light stable as it is hanging over your plants.

STEP 2

Place your gallon jugs with PVC pipes about 4 feet (1.2 m) apart. Insert an S hook and a chain into each end of the PVC pipe and suspend the shop light between the jugs, using additional S hooks and chains. The shop light should hang between the two jugs.

STEP 3

Place the seed tray under the shop light, 1 to 2 inches (2.5 to 5 cm) away from the light. Use shoe boxes or blocks of wood to raise up the seedling trays close to the light. As the plants grow, adjust the height of the trays by removing boxes or blocks of wood so the plants do not touch the light. Adjust the length of the chain to move the light higher or lower, as needed. The seedlings should always be no more than 1 to 2 inches (2.5 to 5 cm) from the light.

SETUP 4: TABLETOP GROW LIGHT

There are many ready-made, small tabletop grow lights available. They require minimal assembly, and they are easy to set up on a table or countertop. A link to my favorite is listed in the Resources section (page 154) at the end of the book.

Advantages

Everything is in the box, including the fixture, lightbulbs, and stand. It takes the guesswork out of what to purchase; no need to shop around for fixtures or bulbs. It's easy to assemble and perfect for a beginning gardener with limited growing space. It also sets up quickly on a table or countertop.

Disadvantages

Much pricier than DIY grow light setups and replacement bulbs can be expensive. However, I've used my tabletop light for several years, and I've never had to replace the bulbs. Depending on which light you purchase, a tabletop light may be limited to a small amount of plants.

How to Set Up a Tabletop Grow Light

STEP 1
Assemble the tabletop light according to the manufacturer's directions.

STEP 2
Place the seed tray under the tabletop light 1 to 2 inches (2.5 to 5 cm) away from the light. Use shoe boxes or blocks of wood to raise up the seedling trays close to the light. As the plants grow, adjust the height of seedling trays by removing boxes or blocks of wood so plants do not touch the light. Adjust the height of the tabletop light by placing blocks of wood under the light stand to move the light higher or lower as needed. The seedlings should always be no more than 1 to 2 inches (2.5 to 5 cm) from the light.

STEP 3
Leave the light on for 24 hours a day until seedlings germinate so they are hit with intense light from the moment of germination. This helps avoid leggy seedlings. Once the seeds germinate, leave the light on for 18 hours a day, off for 6 hours. Plug the light into a timer to turn it on and off automatically.

For my video tutorial on how to set up grow lights, please calikimgardenandhome.com/gardeningvideos. For links to grow light supplies, see the Resources section (page 154) in the back of the book.

THREE COMMON LIGHTING MISTAKES TO AVOID

Problems with indoor seedlings? Ensure healthy, strong indoor seedlings by avoiding these three common lighting mistakes.

MISTAKE 1: SEEDLINGS TOO FAR AWAY FROM THE LIGHT

A common mistake when starting seeds indoors is placing seedlings too far away from the light. This causes them to stretch toward the light, resulting in leggy, thin stems that are too weak to support the plant.

To eliminate this problem and keep your seedlings stocky and strong, place your grow light directly over the seedling tray and keep the seedlings **no more** than 1 to 2 inches (2.5 to 5 cm) away from the light at all times. Check your seedlings daily and adjust the height of the lights or the height of the holding tray as the seedlings grow. Don't allow the seedlings to touch the light, as it may scorch the tender new growth.

MISTAKE 2: NOT ENOUGH LIGHT

The right amount of light is critical to growing vibrant seedlings. Insufficient light will result in leggy seedlings or cause them to be a sickly yellow color rather than a deep, healthy green.

After planting your seeds and placing them under grow lights, leave the lights on 24 hours a day so seedlings are met with a bright, intense light from the moment of germination. This gets them off to a great start from day one.

After seedlings germinate, leave the lights on 18 hours a day and off for 6 hours. Although artificial grow lights mimic sunlight, they are not nearly as intense, and they need to be on for a longer period of time than plants would need to be in sunlight to ensure healthy, green growth.

MISTAKE 3: NOT AUTOMATING

Let's get real. We all get busy. It's easy to forget to turn on (or off) the grow lights. I've done this many times. If you forget to turn your lights on or off, it will affect the growth and health of your seedlings and can cause the dreaded legginess. Do yourself a favor—automate, automate, automate wherever you can, especially when it comes to lighting.

Make it easy on yourself. Hook up a simple, inexpensive timer to your grow lights so you don't have to worry about turning them on and off. The timer will do the work for you. The cost of a timer is money well spent; it helps your seedlings get the proper amount of light so they can grow into vegetables that will give you many harvests.

WATERING AND FERTILIZING INDOOR SEEDLINGS

Hands up if you've ever forgotten to water your plants or if you've "over loved" your plants with too much water and fertilizer. If your hand is up, my hand is held up high right there with you. Watering and fertilizing are where most new gardeners get tripped up. Forget to water and your seedlings are stunted or, worse yet, they die. Too much water or fertilizer can result in mold or waterlogged or burned seedlings.

Consistent watering and fertilizing are key to a productive garden. Especially when seedlings are young, it's vital that they receive regular feedings and stay hydrated. Not getting the consistent nutrients or drying out even once can stunt seedlings and affect future growth.

This section covers exactly how often to water, how much to water, and the best methods to water and fertilize your indoor seedlings so they will flourish and are ready to transplant out in the garden when the time is right.

Watering: How Often?

I wish there was a magic formula for how often to water indoor seedlings. However, watering is dependent on two different variables.

VARIABLE 1: TEMPERATURE

If your seedlings are in a sunny windowsill or in a warm location indoors, they'll dry out quicker and will need watering more often. If they're in a cooler room of the house, they won't dry out as quickly, and they won't need watering as often.

VARIABLE 2: GROWING MEDIUM

Seedlings grown in small 1-inch (2.5 cm) peat pellets will dry out quicker than those grown in the large 3-inch (7.5 cm) peat pellets. Cups with soil or six-pack seed cells will need watering on a different schedule as well.

Sound confusing? It's actually very simple. Two easy watering clues take the guesswork out of it. Check your seedlings daily and look for these clues to monitor their watering needs. In no time,

you'll learn what a seedling that needs water looks and feels like, and you will be watering like a pro.

CLUE 1: COLOR

When the top of the soil in your container or pellet is a dark brown color, this means the soil is moist and doesn't need water. When the top of the soil in your container or pellet turns to a light brown color, this means the soil is starting to dry out and needs water.

CLUE 2: WEIGHT

A container or pellet that does not need water is heavier in weight than a container that is drying out because there is more water content in the soil. A lighter container or pellet has less water content, indicating that it needs water.

On your daily seedling checks, pick up your containers to monitor their weight. When they start to feel lighter and the soil changes to a light brown color, it's time to water. Don't let the soil completely dry out to the point that seedlings are limp and lifeless. Just like us, they need consistent hydration to keep them healthy and prevent them from becoming stressed.

How to Water

Most people water indoor plants by pouring water on the leaves or on the surface of the soil. This method can displace the tiny seeds and damage fragile seedlings, and it is not the most efficient or healthy way to water.

Before your seeds germinate, mist them gently with a spray bottle so the tiny seeds aren't displaced. Once the seeds poke through the soil, even the light mist of a spray bottle can disturb the fragile seedlings. Now is the time to switch to watering from the bottom.

ADVANTAGES OF BOTTOM WATERING

Bottom watering is a healthy, efficient method that allows seedlings to draw moisture into the soil from the bottom up. It has four advantages over watering from the top. First, bottom watering doesn't displace fragile seedings as they grow. Second, it allows the soil to absorb more water by wicking its way up from the bottom to the top, keeping the soil consistently moist so the seedlings don't need to be watered as often. Third, bottom watering allows the plants to develop stronger roots because they are growing down toward the source of the water. Fourth, it's a healthier way to water because it doesn't splash water on the leaves, which could spread diseases from plant to plant.

HOW TO WATER PEAT PELLETS

For watering peat pellets, use a water bottle with a pop-top or a watering can with a spout so the water doesn't splash. Pour water in the bottom of the seedling tray. Let the pellets sit in the water for 5 to 10 minutes. As the pellets absorb the moisture, you will see them turn a darker color from the bottom up as the moisture moves up the pellets. The tops will turn a dark brown color as they fully absorb the moisture. When this happens, carefully pour off the excess water so your plants aren't standing in water. This avoids root rot.

WATERING CONTAINERS WITH SOIL

Your containers with soil all should have drainage holes in the bottom. Pour a few inches of water in the bottom of the tray and place containers in a holding tray. After about 5 to 10 minutes, the top of the soil in the containers will turn a dark brown, indicating the soil has soaked up enough water. Pour off the extra water to avoid root rot.

Fertilizing Seedlings

When your seedlings first start to grow, they have baby leaves, called cotyledons. They don't need extra nutrients until they get to be about 2 inches (5 cm) tall and develop their adult leaves. The adult leaves are called true leaves, and they look like the actual leaf of the veggie. For example, a tomato plant's adult leaves will look and smell like tomato leaves. At this point, they need nutrients to help them grow and flourish.

Fertilize young seedlings with a mild, liquid, organic fertilizer that will not burn your plants. My favorite is VermisTerra worm tea. It's gentle and it provides slow, steady growth for seedlings, and it won't burn them. See the Resources section (page 154) for more information. Worm tea is especially effective in developing the root system of seedlings, and it provides good bacteria to help keep your seedlings vigorous.

"Easy does it" is the key to feeding your young seedlings. Over-fertilizing may burn them and cause stunted growth or yellowing leaves. Use liquid fertilizer at a quarter the strength of the directions on the bottle. If you're using worm tea, mix 1 tablespoon (15 ml) in a half gallon (1.9 L) of water, and use it once a week during a regular watering time.

For my video tutorial on watering and fertilizing seedlings, visit calikimgardenandhome.com/gardeningvideos.

Now that you know how quick and simple it is to start a garden from seed, you're well on your way to growing plenty of tasty organic vegetables and doing it on a budget. Let's talk about what's next in the life of your strong, healthy, vibrant indoor seedlings: transplanting and transitioning your babies to get them ready for the great outdoors.

4

TRANSPLANTING AND TRANSITIONING INDOOR SEEDLINGS TO THE GREAT OUTDOORS

IN HER EXCITEMENT to get her new garden started, Kelly started tomato seeds indoors in early January. In a few weeks, they developed their true leaves, and in a few more weeks, she could see the roots poking out the bottom of the small peat pellets she planted them in. At 4 weeks old, they were several inches tall. Kelly was super excited—they were starting to look and smell like real tomato plants! She couldn't wait to get them planted in her garden bed.

However, she faced a dilemma. Kelly was still 4 weeks away from the last frost date. She couldn't plant her precious tomato seedlings outside yet, because they are a warm-weather vegetable and will die if it frosts. She worked hard to grow her tomato babies from seed and didn't want to risk it. But if they stay in the small peat pellets, they won't have enough room to keep growing healthy and strong until they are ready to plant outside when the weather warms up.

What should Kelly do? It's transplanting time!

In this chapter, we're going to learn how to transplant indoor seedlings into larger containers so they will grow into vibrant, strong plants that are ready to be planted in the garden when the weather is right. We're also going to learn how to transition seedlings to the great outdoors, a process called hardening off.

WHAT IS TRANSPLANTING?

Transplanting is the process of putting your seedlings from one growing container into a larger growing container (also called "up-potting"). Doing so gives them more room to grow. Seedlings that are started indoors may need to be transplanted so they don't get rootbound in their original containers. Larger containers give them room to breathe and will keep them growing until conditions are right for them to thrive in your garden beds.

Not all indoor seedlings will need to be transplanted into larger containers before you move them to their final home in a garden bed. One reason why I like to start seeds for larger vegetables in the large 3-inch (7.5 cm) peat pellets or in small containers with soil is that there is plenty of room for them to grow indoors this way for 6 to 8 weeks. If the weather and soil are warm enough, they can be transplanted directly from the large pellets or small containers into my garden bed, saving me that extra up-potting step while they are growing indoors.

There is not a magic size or a hard-and-fast time frame when you should transplant your seedlings. However, in order to make sure they come through the process with flying colors, the right timing is everything. Transplant them too soon and they could go into transplant shock. Wait too long, they may become stunted and rootbound in their original containers. Not to

worry, with a little practice, moving your young veggies to a new home is easy when you know a few clues to look for to make sure the timing is right.

Clue 1: The Leaves

You'll find the first clue by looking at the leaves. I like to transplant when a seedling has two to three sets of true leaves. Remember, the first leaves to emerge from a seedling are called the cotyledons. These baby leaves provide food for the seedling until the true leaves grow. True leaves are the adult leaves that look like the real vegetable leaf. They will take up nutrients and feed the plant long term. Two to three sets of true leaves are a sign that the seedling is outgrowing its original container and is strong enough to sustain itself in a larger container.

Clue 2: The Roots

Look to the roots for the second clue. When the roots start to poke out the bottom of the pellet or container, the seedling is ready for a larger home. To look at the roots in a small seed-starting container, gently squeeze the bottom of the container, turn it upside down, and hold the stem between two fingers as the seedling is loosened from the container. If the roots are starting to circle around the bottom of the pot, it's ready for a larger home. This is a sign that the roots need more room to take up air, nutrients, and water. A bigger pot will allow the plant to continue growing. If the seedling becomes rootbound it won't be able to take up what it needs and will eventually die.

If you're growing your seedlings in peat pellets, it's time to up-pot when the roots start to grow out of the pellet.

TRANSPLANTING SEEDLINGS INTO LARGER CONTAINERS

Transplanting indoor seedlings is quick and simple, and you may already have some of the supplies around your house. A good rule of thumb is to up-pot your plants into a container that is 25 to 40 percent larger. This gives them room to grow, but it won't overwhelm them by planting them into a container too large for them and risking transplant shock.

Supplies Needed

- Containers of various sizes. Repurpose and upcycle to keep it affordable. Use takeout containers, yogurt or sour cream containers, garden center plastic pots, cardboard seedling pots, and plastic or Styrofoam cups.

- Nail and hammer or a drill for poking drainage holes (if needed)

- Organic bagged potting mix. Do not use outdoor garden soil. It may bring in pests. It is easily compacted, and it is not lightweight enough for growing in containers. See the Resources section (page 154) for my favorite brand.

- Small plastic tub for mixing soil

- Water

- Small shovel

- 2- to 3-inch (5 to 7.5 cm)-deep holding tray for the containers. Repurposed meat trays, foil pans, cookie sheets, or glass casserole dishes work well.

How to Transplant Seedlings

STEP 1
If the containers don't have holes, use a nail or a drill to add three to five drainage holes in the bottom.

STEP 2

Moisten the potting soil in a small plastic tub. Add a small amount of water, then mix it into the soil with a small shovel or trowel. Continue adding water and mixing until the soil is moistened all the way through to the consistency of crumbly brownie mix. There should be no dry soil pockets. Fill the containers about halfway full of the moistened potting soil.

STEP 3

For peat pellets: Carefully peel back the netting on each pellet before transplanting, as the netting restricts the roots.

For seedlings growing in containers: Squeeze the container and carefully turn it upside down, gently grasping the stem between two fingers until the seedling comes loose from the container. You never want to pull the seedling from the stem to get it out of the container, as you may damage the seedling.

STEP 4

For pellets: Place the seedling, pellet end down, into the new container. The top of the seedling should be at the top of the new container. Add more soil underneath the seedling if necessary.

For containers: Place the seedling, soil end down, into the larger container. Add more soil underneath the seedling, if necessary, to bring it up to the top of the container.

STEP 5

Add soil around the seedling until it is level with the top of the new container. Lightly press the soil down so it doesn't have air pockets.

CaliKim's Quick Tip: Tomato Transplanting

When transplanting tomatoes, pinch off the lower leaves and plant the tomato seedling deep in the new container, leaving only the top set of leaves showing over the top of the container whenever possible. A tomato will grow roots wherever it touches the soil: The deeper you plant it, the stronger the plant.

One of the benefits of transplanting is that the new potting mix adds fresh nutrients to your seedlings to take them to the next level of growth and get them ready to plant outside in the garden. I also like to feed my seedlings with worm tea to give them a burst of growth. See Resources (page 154) for my favorite brand.

After they've been up-potted, place the newly transplanted seedling containers into a holding tray. Fill a watering can with water and worm tea or a liquid organic fertilizer; be sure to use half strength (easy does it with seedlings). Add 3

inches (7 cm) of this mixture to the bottom of the holding tray. After 10 minutes, pour off what the containers don't soak up. Feed your plants once a week until they are ready to be planted outside.

For my video tutorial on how to transplant indoor seedlings, please visit calikimgardenandhome.com/gardeningvideos.

TRANSITIONING INDOOR SEEDLINGS TO THE GREAT OUTDOORS

Now that your seedlings are transplanted into new containers, they are ready to move outside to soak up the sunshine, right? Not so fast. I've been there, done that, and can relate to your excitement to get your new plants outdoors. Many a time in my enthusiasm to taste a home-grown tomato, I've rushed my seedlings from growing inside to growing outside too quickly and they have died, unable to handle the quick change from the sheltered environment of indoor growing to the great outdoors.

Knowing when and how to transition your seedlings successfully from growing indoors to growing outdoors is critical to growing them into productive plants. The acclimation process must be done slowly and is called "hardening off."

Moving indoor seedlings to the outdoors is like a baby learning to walk—it should happen gradually. Over time, a baby learns how to move from the protection of a parent's loving arms to navigate those first unsteady steps. At first, a baby holds on to the couch or to mommy's or daddy's hand for a few wobbly steps, then they get stronger and venture farther. Eventually, their

steps become steadier and they can walk across a room on their own. Before you know it, this tiny baby is a toddler, running full steam ahead all by themselves.

In a similar fashion, your indoor seedlings began their lives in a sheltered environment. Light and temperature are regulated. They don't have to face the harsh sunlight, wind, rain, or cold temperatures. They are not ready to go out into the great outdoors all at once; they need your tender loving care to help them do it step by step. Taking the time to transition seedlings to the outdoors gradually helps them acclimate to what they will face in the garden, and they will have a much better chance to survive and thrive.

Hardening off is not difficult and doesn't take a ton of time out of your daily schedule, but it does involve your attention over a week or so.

How to Harden Off Seedlings: Four Easy Steps

STEP 1

Check the frost dates for your area. As a rule, you'll plant your seedlings outside after this date. However, many cool-weather veggies, such as peas, lettuce, kale, and chard, are frost tolerant; they can be planted outside before the last frost date. Warm-weather veggies are not frost tolerant; they should be planted in warm soil. Wait to transition these vegetables and plant them in the garden after the last frost date.

Based on your last frost date, plan when you are going to plant your seedlings outside and start the hardening-off process a week before.

STEP 2

Day 1: Choose the spot for the first hardening-off day. For your seedling's first venture out into the great outdoors, choose a spot in the shade that has protection from the elements. It could be under a tree, on a table on your deck, or under the protection of some type of cover.

Place your seedlings outside in the shady hardening-off spot for an hour or two. They are just getting used to the great outdoors today on their first day out. Make sure your seedlings are not getting battered by the wind, or it is not a day with freezing or extremely hot temperatures. Put them out of reach of your pets or any critters that might wander into your garden. Like you would with a baby learning to walk, keep a watchful eye on your seedlings, making sure they are doing well on their first day out. Bring them in if they start to wilt or if the weather changes suddenly.

After an hour or two, move your plants back inside and place them back under grow lights.

STEP 3

Day 2: Lengthen the hardening-off time. Put your seedlings in the sun for an hour, then move them into the shade for an hour or two, and then move back inside under the grow lights.

STEP 4

Days 3 through 7: Put seedlings outside for an hour or two longer each day, gradually increasing the number of sunlight hours each day until they are in the amount of daily recommended sun for the vegetable that you are growing.

After gradually getting your seedlings acclimated to daytime hours, they will be ready to spend the night in the great outdoors on their own on day 7. Your toddlers are growing into teenagers. It's time to loosen the reins, let go, and let them have a sleepover in the great outdoors. Keep a watchful eye on the temperatures. For heat, protect the seedlings with shade cloth; for frost, bring them indoors.

Once your seedlings spend the entire night outside, they are ready to be planted in the garden.

For my video tutorial on how to acclimate indoor seedlings to outdoors, please visit calikimgardenandhome.com/gardeningvideos.

The hardening-off period is a good time to choose the placement of your garden. You can begin preparing your garden bed for planting so that when your seedlings are ready, your garden is ready to roll. You'll be one step closer to harvesting your own fresh, mouthwatering veggies.

Are you ready to get your hands in the soil and feel the warm sun on your back?

Let's dig in.

5

PLACEMENT OF YOUR GARDEN AND HOW TO PREP IT FOR PLANTING

CHOOSING THE PLACEMENT of your garden space is not as tricky as you might think. It's not rocket science, and it doesn't take a lot of time. But it is something you'll want to decide before you start dropping seeds in the soil. No worries, even if you have never planted a garden before, the tips in this chapter, along with a little bit of good ol' common sense and observation, will make it easy for you to pick the space where your veggie garden will thrive.

Let's walk around your outdoor space together and scope out the potential spots, shall we? While we are strolling, let's talk about three things to look for when deciding the placement of your garden: proximity to your house, water source, and sun exposure. I'll also share three popular methods—containers, raised beds, and in-ground gardens —and the pros and cons of each for growing your delicious veggies. Last but not least: The secret is in the prep! I'll share how to prepare your garden for planting in a downright quick and simple way, no matter what method you are using to grow your beautiful, organic garden.

Ready to pick a spot where your garden dreams will come true?

Keep It Close

As we step outside your door, let's keep your garden beds and containers as close to your house as possible, shall we? You will get a thrill every time you see those beautiful vegetables from your window, and when your garden grocery store is close to your kitchen, you're more likely to step outside and grab veggies for a meal. It's super handy and fun to grow a container or two of your favorite herbs within snipping distance of your grill as you fire it up for a quick summer barbecue. With your garden close to your house, maintenance is easier and you're more likely to spot any issues that need your immediate attention before they get out of hand.

If you don't have a yard, you have it easy! Your garden will always be nearby, growing in containers on your deck or balcony. It will be quick to grab veggies for a meal and easy to keep up.

Sun Exposure

As we continue our stroll, let's look for a spot that balances proximity to your house with sunshine. Sun is the most important component to growing lots of veggies—the more the merrier! Most fruiting vegetables (e.g., tomatoes, peppers, beans, squash, cucumbers, eggplant) need full sun—at least 6 hours of direct sun a day. Many will be more productive in 8 to 10 hours of sun a day.

With a little observation, it's easy to determine if a potential garden site has enough light. Depending on the direction your outdoor space

is facing in relation to your house, trees, or other buildings, we may need to walk 6 to 8 feet (1.8 to 2.4 m) or so from your house (if your outdoor space allows) to find the best spot. Stake off a 4 × 8 foot (1.2 × 2.4 m) section of your yard; this is the size of a typical garden bed.

Observe this space throughout the day. Note when and where the shadows from your house, trees, fence, or other nearby buildings fall on that spot, and how many hours of sunlight it receives during the day. Keep in mind, the 6 hours of sunlight doesn't have to be in consecutive hours. If this location gets 3 hours of sun in the morning, is shaded midday, and gets 3 hours of sun later in the afternoon, you've found your sweet garden spot!

Don't have a large sunny spot? You can still grow veggies with a less-than-perfect location. I like to have multiple garden spaces with varying amounts of sunlight to match the vegetables that I am growing. Smaller varieties of tomatoes, lettuce, spinach, kale, chard, and other leafy vegetables do well in partial sun—3 hours of sunlight. In fact, the shade will protect cool-weather greens in the heat of the summer. Tuck in veggies wherever you can.

Keep in mind that in the fall and winter months, the sun will be lower in the sky and the shadows will be longer, so you may have more shade in your garden space. During the summer when the sun is higher in the sky, the shadows are shorter, and the same spot may be in full sun. For example, my garden is on the north side of my house, in full sun during the summer but almost entirely shaded by our house during the winter months. This affects the varieties of vegetables that will grow best during specific times of the year. See Appendix 1 and 2 (pages 149–151) for sunlight needs of specific vegetables.

If you live in the Northern Hemisphere, ideally you want to situate your garden from north to south for the most sun exposure. Plant the tallest veggies (e.g., full-sized tomatoes, corn, plants on trellises) on the back (north) side of your garden bed so they don't shade out the smaller plants that you will plant in the front (south) side of your garden. Southern Hemisphere gardeners will plant in the reverse: Orient your garden bed from south to north, with the tallest plants on the south side and the shortest plants on the north side.

DRIP IRRIGATION

Drip irrigation is optional but recommended. If you plan to use it, the easiest time to install it is after prepping the soil in your in-ground garden, raised bed, or container, but **before** you plant your seeds or seedlings. This way, you can plant your veggies next to the drip-irrigation emitters for maximum watering and growth, and you won't disturb your plants by installing drip irrigation later in the growing season. I recommend a separate drip-irrigation system for containers, as they have different watering needs than in-ground gardens or raised beds. See Chapter 6 for more on setting up a drip-irrigation system.

CLOSE TO A WATER SOURCE

As we walk along, show me where your water source is. Let's plant your garden as close to it as possible. Consistent watering means a productive garden. Make it easy on yourself. If possible, plant your garden near a hose bib so you don't have to haul watering cans or string hoses or sprinklers around your yard. This makes it easier to install drip irrigation, a huge time and water saver (see Chapter 6).

HOW WILL YOUR GARDEN GROW?

Now that we've chosen the sweet spot(s) for your garden, would you like to grow your garden in raised beds, in containers, or a combo? Each method has its advantages and disadvantages. One of the aspects of gardening that I love is that there are many ways to get the same results. Do what works best for you! Remember, this is your garden. How and where you grow it depends on your space, growing conditions, the needs of your family, the time and money you have, and what you like to do!

IT'S ALL IN THE SOIL

The biggest investment you'll make when starting a garden is in the soil. Growing a garden in soil packed full of organic matter and nutrients goes a long way toward growing plants that are healthy, productive, and able to stand up to the elements, pests, and diseases.

Soil is a living, breathing organism. Like you and I, soil needs to be fed on a regular basis to be healthy and productive. One of the best methods to feed your garden soil for free is by making compost and adding it to your soil on a regular basis. Turn your kitchen scraps, shredded leaves, grass clippings, and yard waste into "black gold" to feed your garden beds or containers.

Making compost is a relatively easy process, but it does take time. When you are starting out, an initial investment in premade compost, garden soil, and amendments may be needed. Whether you are purchasing soil for containers or a raised bed, or you're amending the native soil of your in-ground garden, purchase the best quality organic soil or compost you

can afford. Your garden will reward you many times over! Don't skimp on the soil, as you'll pay for it down the road in the form of a less productive garden.

Bagged organic garden soil, potting mix, and compost are usually available at your local garden center or from online sources. See the Resources section (page 154) for my favorite bagged soil. A good garden soil or potting mix will be light and fluffy, and it is not easily compacted—veggie roots need to breathe. It will retain water well, and it should be full of organic material and nutrient dense.

In some areas, organic soil may be available in bulk from a local landscape company for a fraction of the cost of bagged soil at garden centers. If you have access to a truck, or you have a friend who can split a load with you, this is an economical option.

Advantages

The best way to garden on the cheap is to plant directly in the ground. An in-ground garden is a great option if you have a large sunny spot with well-draining, or even average, soil. In-ground gardening keeps your expenses down because you'll make use of the existing soil. This method doesn't require building anything; there's no need to spend precious funds on materials for a raised bed. No special tools are required aside from a shovel or two and a willingness to work hard. The money you save can be used for seeds, trellises, organic amendments, fertilizer, and compost (or make your own for free). An in-ground garden provides flexibility for oddly shaped areas where raised beds will not fit.

Disadvantages

Although it's a great way to garden on a budget, an in-ground garden bed initially takes an investment of time and effort to dig out. This could be difficult for gardeners with a busy schedule or physical challenges. It's more challenging to control weeds with this method, as native soil typically has a multitude of weed seeds that will persistently try to crowd out your veggies.

Unless you have beautiful, loose, fertile soil (unusual for a first garden), you will need to add a significant amount of compost and/or soil amendments. The soil may take 2 to 3 years to reach its maximum potential. It can also be hard on the back and knees, as in-ground gardens require bending and stooping.

IN-GROUND GARDEN BEDS

The day we moved into our house, I laid eyes on my first garden space—what a thrill! It was a weedy, grassy corner of our backyard, and I knew it would be a lot of hard work to turn it into a space that would grow beautiful organic veggies. I didn't have the money or the know-how to construct raised beds and fill them with soil, but I wasn't afraid of good old hard work. I borrowed a rototiller from a friend and jumped in. Visions of fully loaded tomato, pepper, and cucumber plants along with rows of leafy greens kept me pushing that rototiller in the hot sun. Before I knew it, my precious garden space was carved out.

How to Prep an In-Ground Garden Bed for Planting: Three Easy Steps

STEP 1
Loosen the soil in the planting area with a shovel or pitchfork.

STEP 2
Remove any obstructions from the soil, such as grass, weeds, and rocks. Break up large chunks of soil with your shovel or pitchfork until the soil is loose.

STEP 3
Add amendments to your soil so your seedlings have the nutrients they need to get off to a great start. Add compost to cover the garden bed 2 to 3 inches (5 to 7.5 cm) deep. Work it into the top 6 inches (14 cm) of the soil with a pitchfork. If your budget allows, add worm castings (see Resources, page 154) to the entire garden bed and work it in with the compost. Worm castings will supercharge your soil with beneficial bacteria and microbes; this will help protect your plants against disease and pests. For a budget-friendly alternative, only add worm castings to each planting hole around the roots of your plants (see Chapter 7, Planting Vegetable Seedlings in the Garden).

If the soil is dry, add water as you are working in the compost and worm castings, but not too much. You don't want the soil to be muddy or dripping with moisture or your new plants or seeds will rot when planted. The soil should be evenly moist; the consistency of crumbly brownie mix.

Whew, we just got a great workout and saved a ton of money in the process. Who said gardening isn't good exercise? Now you are ready to plant your veggies!

For my video tutorial on how to prepare a garden bed for planting vegetables, please visit calikimgardenandhome.com/gardeningvideos.

RAISED BEDS

A second way to grow your veggies is in a raised bed. A raised bed is a garden box that is placed in a sunny spot in your garden or on a deck or patio and filled with purchased soil. They can be placed over existing soil, native grass, concrete, or stone. There are many premade raised beds on the market or you can make your own. They're super easy and inexpensive to make. Using repurposed materials, such as old fence slats, scrap wood, or reused stone blocks, keeps it even more budget friendly.

The most common size for raised beds is 4 × 8 feet (1.2 × 2.4 m). This size allows you to be able to reach to the middle of the garden bed from either side to tend your veggies. Build it smaller—for example, 4 × 4 feet (1.2 × 1.2 m) or 2 × 4 feet (0.6 × 1.2 m)—to fit whatever space you have available in your yard, or on your deck or patio.

Advantages

Raised beds are easy to build, and they provide structure to your garden. Depending on the material they are made with, they can provide color, texture, and beauty to your garden. They are a fantastic option if you have native soil that is heavy clay or full of rocks. This type of soil can be hard to dig, require a lot of amendments, and sometimes takes 2 to 3 years to reach its full potential.

A huge advantage to raised beds is that setting them up requires minimal digging. This is a big plus if you don't have the time to dig out an in-ground garden, have compacted, hard-to-dig soil, or have physical challenges. Raised beds can be set up anywhere, over existing soil, grass, or even on top of concrete. Once a raised bed is set up, just fill with soil, add drip irrigation (optional), and plant your garden.

Because the raised bed will be filled with purchased soil that is chock full of organic nutrients, the veggies will have the energy they need to be productive right away. The soil in a raised bed will be relatively free of weeds usually found in native garden soil, and maintenance will be a breeze. Depending on the height of the beds, gardening in raised beds saves on kneeling and bending over, and it is easier on your back.

Raised beds are especially effective when growing root veggies, such as carrots, beets, and

potatoes, as these veggies love the loose soil and grow beautifully with no roots or rocks to obstruct their growth.

Disadvantages

Although raised beds are easy to maintain, the biggest disadvantage is the cost. Building your own is inexpensive, depending on the type of materials used, but purchasing premade raised beds can be costly. Soil to fill a raised bed will by far be the biggest expense.

How to Build an Easy, Inexpensive Raised Bed and Prep It for Planting

This project works best if you enlist the help of a family member or friend. One of the rewards of gardening is sharing the fun!

Supplies Needed

(To build a 4 × 4-foot [1.2 × 1.2 m] raised bed; adjust to fit your space.)

- Four 4 foot × 2 inch × 12 inch (1.2 m × 5 cm × 30 cm) planks of wood. These will be the sides of the raised bed. Many hardware stores will cut the wood for you. Untreated pine or Douglas fir is inexpensive; cedar and redwood are more rot resistant but also more expensive.

- Four 12-inch (30 cm) pieces of a 2 × 4 (5 × 10 cm) plank: These will be the corner braces to stabilize the sides of raised bed.

- 25–30 (3-inch or 7.5 cm) deck screws

- Cardboard

- Garden soil. You will need about 16 cubic feet to fill a 4 × 4 foot (1.2 × 1.2 m) raised bed.

TOOLS
- Drill with Phillips head drill bit

- Saw, if you are cutting the wood

- Rake

STEP 1

Attach the 12-inch (30 cm) corner braces and two 4-foot (1.2 m) planks: Place a 12-inch (30 cm) corner brace on top of one of the 4-foot (1.2 m) planks, flush with the end. Place a screw ½ inch (1 cm) from the top edge of the corner brace. Drill the screw into the wood to attach it to the 4-foot (1.2 m) plank. Place the second screw ½ inch (1 cm) from the bottom edge of the corner brace. Drill the screw into the wood to attach it to the 4-foot (1.2 m) plank. Repeat this process for the other end of the same 4-foot plank and again with a second 4-foot (1.2 m) plank.

STEP 2

Attach the sides: With a friend's help, take one end of one 4-foot plank with the corner brace attached. Line it up at a 90-degree angle with the end of a second 4-foot (1.2 m) plank without the corner brace attached. The plank without the corner brace should be on the outside. Attach the two pieces with two screws. Repeat this process with the other two 4-foot (1.2 m) planks, and then again to connect all four sides of the garden bed.

STEP 3

Place your new raised bed in your garden space. Line the inside with flattened cardboard boxes, completely covering the ground underneath. This limits weeds from growing through into your raised bed. If your raised bed will be placed on concrete, you can skip this step.

STEP 4

Fill your new raised bed to the top with soil. Use a rake to level out the soil.

Wasn't that super quick, simple, and inexpensive to build? Now you are ready to plant your veggies in your new raised bed.

CONTAINERS

Don't think that because you are short on space you can't grow your own organic veggies. Not so. Nearly any veggie that can be grown in a garden bed can be grown in a container on a deck, patio, or balcony. Containers are also a good option to expand your growing space, even if you already have an in-ground garden or raised beds. Use containers that fit the space you *do* have, and grow up whenever possible, using trellises, stacked crates, deck rails, or fences to maximize your growing space and sunlight.

½ gallon [1.9 L]; or smaller up to 1,000+ gallons [3,785 L]), and colors. Fill an entire patio full of container-friendly veggies. Or tuck one or two containers of veggies or herbs near your back door, or near your kitchen or grill. Or place a few near your garden beds to expand your growing space.

I prefer to grow in durable fabric containers over plastic. See the Resources section (page 154) for my favorite. Plants growing in plastic containers tend to overheat in hot weather. Fabric containers are porous, providing drainage and keeping the plants cooler in hot weather. The airflow allows the roots to "air prune." This is when the roots form a fibrous mass, rather than wrapping around the plant or becoming rootbound as they tend to do in plastic or ceramic containers. This fibrous root mass is still able to take up moisture and nutrients (not the case in a rootbound plant), and the plant will be healthier and more productive.

PORTABILITY

Growing in containers allows you to have a portable garden. Containers can be moved around your patio; use a plant dolly for large containers. Place your plants at various locations in your yard to change it up and expand your growing space; you can also chase the sun or easily move your plants into shade when needed.

EASY TO PLANT AND MAINTAIN

Setting up containers is by far the quickest and simplest method to grow veggies. Just pick up a container and fill it with soil, seeds, and plants.

Advantages

The advantages to growing in containers are versatility, portability, and ease of planting.

VERSATILITY

You can easily find a container to fit whatever space you have to grow in, no matter how little or how much space you have. Containers come in all types (e.g., plastic, ceramic, fabric), shapes (e.g., round, square, rectangular), sizes (e.g.,

Add water and you have an instant garden. Maintenance is a piece of cake: You are using purchased potting mix. There are no weeds to deal with. And you can plant only the containers you have time and energy to keep up with.

Like raised beds, containers are especially effective for growing root veggies, such as carrots, beets, and potatoes. These veggies need loose soil and good drainage, and they grow beautifully with no roots or rocks to obstruct their growth.

Disadvantages

The biggest disadvantage of containers is the cost of containers and soil. Keep costs down by picking containers up at thrift stores and garage sales. Get creative, upcycle, reuse, repurpose, think outside of the box. Use a 5-gallon (19-L) bucket from the hardware store or repurpose an old kitchen trash can or a storage bin. Organic potting mix to fill your containers will by far be the biggest expense. Depending on how many containers you have to fill, reduce costs by purchasing potting mix in bulk or make your own.

Another disadvantage to growing in containers is that soil dries out quicker, and nutrients drain faster. They will need watered and fertilized more often than raised beds or in-ground gardens.

How to Prep Containers for Planting Veggies

STEP 1

Choose a container. Large veggies (e.g., full-sized tomatoes, squash, eggplant, cucumbers) will need a larger container. Choose a 15- to 20-gallon (57 to 76 L) container for the best production. Small- or medium-sized veggies (e.g., compact veggie varieties, dwarf tomatoes, peppers, peas, root veggies, lettuce, greens, herbs) can be grown in a smaller container. For these, choose a 3- to 15-gallon (11 to 57 L) container.

STEP 2

Fill the container with potting mix. Most bagged potting mixes come dry. Moisten the mix so your plants have the water they need to get off to a good start. Add potting mix to the container a little at a time, watering and working the moisture into the soil with a shovel as you fill the container. Soil should be evenly moist throughout—not waterlogged. You are looking for the consistency of crumbly brownie mix.

Visit calikimgardenandhome.com/gardeningvideos for my video tutorials on how to grow veggies in containers.

Ready to Grow

Now that you have your in-ground garden, raised beds, and/or containers prepped for planting, you are ready plant your seedlings or seeds into their new garden home. This is the fun part. It's what you've been waiting for from the moment you started those seeds indoors weeks ago. What an exciting day! (See Chapter 7, Planting Vegetable Seedlings in the Garden).

But first, let's talk about watering—the key to a productive garden.

6

WATERING—THE KEY TO A PRODUCTIVE GARDEN

MARY JO'S FIRST ATTEMPT at growing veggies didn't work. Her garden died before she harvested anything. When I asked her what happened, her answer was one I had, unfortunately, heard before. "I just wanted to quickly and easily grow veggies for my family. I planted my seedings and couldn't wait for harvest day. However, I had no idea how to take care of my garden and was spending a lot of time watering during the hot summer. I became overwhelmed, and my garden died before I could figure out how to streamline this process. I got discouraged and quit. I figured I just didn't have time to grow my own food."

Now that you have your seedlings growing strong and your garden bed ready to plant, it's time to consider one of the most important factors to the success of an organic vegetable garden: watering. It's the number one area where new gardeners get tripped up the most.

information you need to water your veggies effectively and efficiently. Knowing when, how often, and how much to water your garden can make the difference between a thriving garden that provides lots of yummy veggies or stunted plants that die before you harvest anything.

WHEN SHOULD YOU WATER?

During the hot summer months, avoid watering in the heat of the day. Water in the morning or evening in the cool of the day. This reduces water evaporation and makes the water available for your plant when it needs it the most—during the hottest part of the day.

WHERE SHOULD YOU WATER?

Water at the base of your plants whenever possible so the water gets to where it needs to go—the roots. Overhead watering increases the chance of your plants getting fungal leaf diseases, and often water evaporates before it gets to the roots. Keeping your plant leaves as dry as possible helps control common garden diseases, such as powdery mildew, blight, leaf spot, and many more.

HOW MUCH SHOULD YOU WATER?

Different vegetables vary in their watering needs. Most plants need about ¾ gallon (2.8 L) of water per plant per week, or more if the weather is over 90°F (32°C). Container plants will dry out quicker and need more water, sometimes daily in hot weather. Water containers until the water runs out the bottom. Monitor the soil moisture to see how often you need to water your garden beds or containers.

Consistent watering is the key to a productive garden. Some gardeners are fortunate enough to live where it rains regularly, and they don't have to worry about watering. Here in Southern California, it rarely rains during the summer, so watering my garden is a huge issue for me and can eat up a ton of time.

"How much water does my garden need?" is a question I get asked over and over again. Forget to water and you end up with dead plants. Water too much and you get plants that are water-logged with rotting roots and prone to disease.

There is no need to guess how to water your garden. This chapter will give you all the

HOW OFTEN SHOULD YOU WATER?

The frequency of watering depends on the weather. In hot, dry weather, the soil will dry out quicker and you'll have to water more often than you would in cold or rainy weather.

The most important thing you can do for the welfare of your garden during the hot summer days is to check the moisture level of your soil frequently to determine whether you need to water your garden. This is very easy to do either with a moisture meter or with your finger.

Most moisture meters can be calibrated according to the ideal moisture for the type of soil in your garden. Put the probe of the moisture meter into the soil. If the moisture meter shows that your soil is wet, you don't need to water. If it shows that your soil is dry, give your plants a drink.

To check soil moisture with your finger, simply stick your finger in the soil as far as you can reach it at the base of your plants. If the soil feels wet, you don't need to water. If it feels dry, water your plants.

HOW SHOULD YOU WATER YOUR GARDEN?

Rather than quick watering sessions, water your garden less frequently, but water slowly, deeply, and for longer periods of time. Deep watering encourages the plant to stretch its roots down to take up water and nutrients, and it allows you to go longer between waterings. The deeper the roots, the stronger, sturdier, and more productive the plant will be. More roots equals more fruit (or veggies) and a happy gardener.

If you are using a watering can or a hose and nozzle, water slowly at the base of your plants and let the water sink in. Then repeat, letting the water sink in again so it gets all the way to the roots.

For my video tutorial on how to water your garden, please visit calikimgardenandhome.com/gardeningvideos.

MULCH, MULCH, MULCH

Mulch is a layer of organic material, such as shredded leaves or straw, spread over the soil around your plants. One of the biggest benefits of mulch is it keeps moisture in the soil and you'll have to water less. I mulch every time I plant anything; it's critical to the well-being of my garden, especially in the hot, dry summers.

FOUR BENEFITS OF MULCH

- Breaks down over time, adding organic matter to the soil, aerating it, and making it more fertile.

- Reduces water evaporation, which means you'll be watering less.

- Keeps roots warmer in cold temperatures and cooler in warm temperatures.

- Brings in the worms like crazy. Worms aerate and break up heavy clay soil and leave free fertilizer behind in the form of worm poop (or worm castings).

HOW TO MULCH

After planting seedlings, spread a 2- to 3-inch (5 to 7.5 cm) layer of shredded leaves or straw at the base of the plant. When planting seeds, spread just an inch (2.5 cm) of mulch over the planting area so the seedlings can easily germinate. Add more mulch to get to that 2- to 3-inch (5 to 7.5 cm) layer of thickness as plants grow.

If you have enough mulch, spread it in a thick layer over your entire garden bed. Mulching garden beds at the end of the fall before winter hits is an excellent way to get your garden beds ready for spring. The moisture of the winter rain and snow will help break down the mulch and add much-needed organic matter to your soil, giving you a jump when you are ready to plant your garden again in the spring.

WANT SOME TIME BACK? AUTOMATE WITH DRIP IRRIGATION

Watering your garden can be a huge task, and it can eat up a lot of time. Let's face it, most of us lead busy lives and don't have time to hand water our backyard veggie patch with the garden hose. Some days watering is just not a priority, and when your plants don't get the water they need, they don't produce well for you. Or worse yet, they will die.

My favorite way to water is with a drip irrigation system because it saves water and a ton of time, and the slow, steady drip sinks deep into the roots of your plants.

I've used drip irrigation in my garden for years. It's quick and simple to install, inexpensive, and gets the water to where it needs to go. This translates into lots of delicious and nutritious veggies for my family to eat. If you are a busy person who is always looking for ways to do more with less, like I am, drip irrigation is an excellent option for watering your garden.

Once I showed my friend Mary Jo how to install drip irrigation in her garden and automate it with a timer, growing her own food wasn't so time consuming, and it became an enjoyable activity she could fit into her busy schedule. She now has a thriving, productive garden that she harvests vegetables from daily to feed her family.

What Is Drip Irrigation?

Drip irrigation is a method of watering your garden through a network of hoses, tubes, and emitters. The water flows from a hose bib or sprinkler valve and is distributed to the garden bed so you can water multiple plants at once. Hoses with drip emitters are placed directly at the base of the plant and allow the water to drip out slowly. Drip irrigation is easy to install, and it's low-cost. It also can be easily connected to a timer for automated watering of your entire garden.

SIX BENEFITS OF DRIP IRRIGATION

GETS WATER TO THE ROOTS

Drip irrigation allows the water to seep slowly deep into the soil, feeding the root zone where the plants need it the most. Healthy roots equal healthy plants, and healthy plants means more veggies.

SAVES WATER AND MONEY

Drip irrigation saves water and minimizes evaporation. The water drips directly into the soil instead of sitting on the surface of the plants where it can quickly evaporate. This means you are using less water (a cost savings on your water bill) while getting better results.

VERSATILITY

Whether you need water for plants in containers, raised beds, an in-ground garden, a balcony, or a large or small garden, drip irrigation is up for the job. A drip irrigation system can be used anywhere in your garden, and it is easy to expand as you add additional growing space. I recommend a separate drip irrigation system for containers, as they dry out quicker and need watered more often than an in-ground garden or raised bed.

For my video tutorial on how to install drip irrigation in containers, please visit calikimgardenandhome.com/gardeningvideos.

REDUCES DISEASE

Water that sits on the surface of your plants can encourage diseases, such as powdery mildew and blight, to spread quickly through your garden. Because drip irrigation targets the roots of your plants, it reduces diseases and fungal growth.

SAVES TIME

Drip irrigation is a huge time saver. I'd be lost without it. As a general rule, if I can't get water to an area via drip irrigation, I don't plant in that location. I know myself. I have kids to get to school, loved ones I want to spend time with, a garden to maintain, videos to film, blog posts to write, dinner to make, and the list goes on. Hand watering is simply not something I have time to do. Drip irrigation takes the guesswork out of it and gives me time back—a win-win all the way around.

QUICK, EASY, INEXPENSIVE INSTALLATION

Many people are intimidated by the thought of installing a drip irrigation system, but there's no need to be. Drip irrigation is quick to install. As a newbie gardener, I started with a simple drip irrigation raised bed kit. See the Resources section (page 154) for my favorite kit. I found it very easy get up and running in a short period of time. Over the years, I've added to my system to accommodate my expanding garden.

Your drip system should be installed after you've prepped your garden bed or container for planting but before you plant your seedlings. This way as soon as your veggies are planted, they have the water they need, and you won't disturb them by installing the drip irrigation system after they are planted.

Starting with a drip irrigation kit takes the guesswork out of installation, as it has many of the parts you need for a basic drip system for a garden bed or container. The parts that come in the kit can also be purchased separately for later expansion of your system.

Drip irrigation can be connected to a hose bib or to a sprinkler system. The following steps are for connecting it to a hose bib.

HOW TO INSTALL DRIP IRRIGATION TO A HOSE BIB

SWIVEL ADAPTOR

PRESSURE REGULATOR

SCREEN FILTER

STEP 1

There are three options when starting the install:

Option 1: Install the drip system directly to your hose bib.

Option 2: If your hose bib is not near your garden bed(s), connect a heavy-duty hose to the hose bib, and run the heavy-duty hose to your garden bed. With this option, the drip irrigation system will be connected to the end of the heavy-duty hose closest to your garden bed(s).

Option 3: Connect a timer to your hose bib or hose to automate your drip irrigation system.

See the section later in this chapter about the benefits of automating with a timer. With this option, the drip system will then be connected to the opposite end of the timer and installed in your garden beds.

STEP 2

All parts are included in the drip irrigation kit unless otherwise noted.

A screen filter is optional but highly recommended, as it filters out debris that might plug up the system. Screw the screen filter (purchased separately; see Resources, page 154) directly to the hose bib, heavy-duty hose, or timer, depending on which option works best for you.

STEP 3

Screw the 25-psi (1.7 bar) pressure regulator on to the other end of the screen filter. This lowers the water pressure for optimal functioning of the system. The drip system works best at 25 psi (1.7 bar); a garden hose has water coming out at a pressure of around 60 psi (4 bar).

STEP 4

Connect the swivel adaptor (in the kit) to the end of the pressure regulator.

STEP 5

The end of the swivel adaptor has a compression fitting. Connect the ½-inch (1 cm) poly tubing supply line to the compression fitting end by wiggling it back and forth until it snuggly fits into the compression fitting. Run the ½-inch (1 cm) poly tubing supply line along the one end of your garden bed, securing by pushing with landscape staples into the soil.

STEP 6

Cut the ½-inch (1 cm) tubing to fit the width of one end of the garden bed, pinch the end of the ½-inch (1 cm) tubing, and secure with a figure 8 fastener so the water doesn't run out the end. If you have other garden beds to irrigate, continue the ½-inch (1 cm) supply line to another garden bed nearby and install in that garden bed as well (following the steps below).

STEP 7

Install the ¼-inch (6 mm) drip emitter tubing to the ½-inch (1 cm) supply line tubing. To do this, first punch holes with the hole punch tool every 6 inches (15 cm) in the supply line that runs along the end of your garden bed.

STEP 8

Push one end of a double-ended barbed connector into the end of the ¼-inch (6 mm) drip emitter tubing line. Push the other end of the barbed connector into one of the holes in the ½-inch (1 cm) supply line. Wiggle the barbed connector back and forth into the hole in the supply line until it clicks into place.

If you have a hard time getting the connectors to snap into place, heat the end of the hose or connectors up for a few seconds with a fireplace lighter to soften them and the parts will snap right into place.

STEP 9

Connect a length of ¼-inch (6 mm) drip emitter tubing to the other end of the barbed connector and run the drip emitter tubing down the length of the garden bed. Secure the ¼-inch (6 mm) drip emitter tubing to the soil with landscape staples.

STEP 10

Cut the ¼-inch (6 mm) drip emitter line to fit the length of the garden bed and put a "goof plug" at the end to prevent water from running out the end.

STEP 11

Repeat steps 6 through 11 every 6 inches (15 cm) along the ½-inch (1 cm) supply line so that the garden bed gets adequate water coverage.

For my video tutorial on how to install drip irrigation in your garden beds, please visit calikimgardenandhome.com/gardeningvideos.

How Often to Water with Drip Irrigation

When you first install drip irrigation in your garden, it will be a trial-and-error process to determine how long and how often to water. The amount of time to run your system and the number of days between watering (frequency) will depend on how far apart your drip emitters are spaced, how many gallons per hour (GPH) of water each emitter puts out, and what type of soil you have.

Start out by running your system for 30 minutes, then check your soil with a moisture meter or with your finger to see how wet it is. If the soil is still dry, run the drip system longer. If it is evenly moist, you are good to go. Check the soil daily until you find how many days it takes for your soil to begin to dry out and run your system again. Check your garden more often during heat waves as you may need to water for an extra cycle. Once you have completed the initial trial-and-error period, run your drip system (or set your timer if you are using a timer) for the length and frequency that works for your garden.

Automate with a Timer—Set It and Forget It

I highly recommend automating your system with a timer. We gardeners need to be able to "set it and forget it." Although it is a simple task to go outside and turn on the faucet to run the drip irrigation for my garden, I know myself. I will forget. I won't get to it. Or worse, I will turn it on and forget to turn it off.

A timer for your drip irrigation system provides consistent watering (a must), gives you time back, *and* gives you peace of mind knowing your garden is getting the regular moisture it needs to grow lots of veggies.

If you choose this option, simply screw your timer directly onto your hose bib or the end of a heavy-duty hose, then install the drip irrigation system with the steps above. I use a simple solar

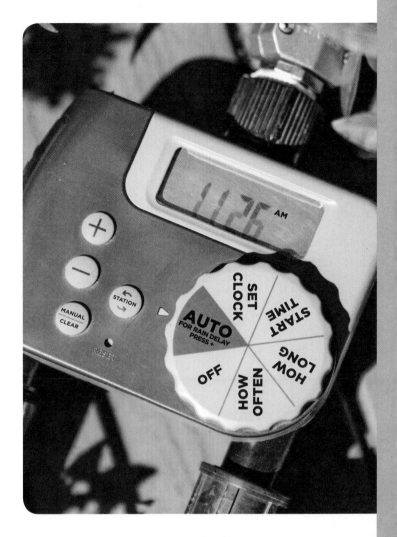

powered hose-end timer. There are many options for timers on the market that allow you to set up multiple watering zones in your garden for added flexibility. See Resources (page 154) for my favorite.

For my video tutorial on how to install a timer to automate your drip irrigation system, please visit calikimgardenandhome.com/gardeningvideos.

You've put a lot of time into growing your seedlings. Consistent watering will protect your investment, take the guesswork out of watering, and reward you with lots of tasty veggies.

Next stop? Let's get your garden planted!

7

PLANTING VEGETABLE SEEDLINGS IN THE GARDEN

TODAY IS THE DAY. The weather is getting warmer, and the last frost date has passed. Your indoor seedlings are hardened off and ready to be planted outside. Your garden bed is prepped, and the drip irrigation is in place. It's planting day, and you are one step closer to eating your own homegrown, mouthwatering vegetables and making your dream of an organic garden a reality.

If you are like me when I planted my first garden, you have a ton of questions. How deep should I plant my tomato seedlings? What's the correct spacing for my peppers? How much sunlight do cucumbers need? Does my squash need a trellis? How much should I water and fertilize my plants?

Question no more! Let's take the guesswork out of it so you don't have to wonder how to plant your vegetable seedlings in the garden. In this chapter, you'll learn the general as well as the specific. I'll share the basics of both warm- and cool-weather veggies, including the temperature, sunlight, water, and fertilizer they need to grow best and produce to their potential.

We'll also walk step by step through specific, nitty-gritty details of how to plant popular warm- and cool-weather veggies, how deep and far apart to space them, and which ones can be direct seeded or grow best from transplants. We'll talk about which plants need the support of a cage or trellis, and I share my favorite quick, simple, and inexpensive (or free) trellis ideas.

All along the way, I'll share tips and tricks to keep the planting process quick, easy, and cost effective. Even with no prior experience, you'll feel confident that you can get your garden planted and grow a beautiful variety of fresh veggies that you'll be proud to bring to the table.

WARM-WEATHER VEGETABLES

The long, sunny days of summer are perfect for growing classic warm-weather veggies, such as tomatoes, peppers, cucumbers, squash, eggplant, beans, and corn. Make sure to take a lot of

pictures of your baby seedlings, because from this point forward, with lots of heat and sunshine, they'll be growing at warp speed, and you'll be enjoying summer veggies in just a few months.

When to Plant Warm-Weather Veggies Outdoors

Warm-weather veggies can be planted outdoors after the last frost date in your area. They thrive in nighttime temperatures of 60–75°F (15–23°C) and daytime temperatures of 75–90°F (23–32°C). Cool temperatures (less than 60°F/15°C) or overly hot temperatures (more than 90°F/32°C) slow their growth. Warm-weather veggies are cold sensitive, and in most cases, frost will kill the plant.

If you plant outside too early or an unexpected frost is predicted, protect your seedlings during cold nights. Put four stakes in the ground around your seedling and drape a blanket over the stakes. For small seedlings, cover them with a plastic storage bin or milk jug with the bottom cut out. Remove the cover during the day when the sun is out and the temperatures are above freezing so the seedlings don't overheat under the cover.

Sunlight Needs for Warm-Weather Veggies

Warm-weather veggies are sun lovers. Plant them where they get full sun—at least 6 hours of sun a day, more is better. Smaller vegetable varieties, such as cherry tomatoes or pattypan squash, will produce with 6 hours of sun a day, but the larger vegetables varieties will need 8 to 10 hours of sun for the best production.

Watering and Fertilizing Warm-Weather Veggies

If you want to grow lots of veggies, the key is to water them consistently (see Chapter 6). You also need to feed them powerful, organic nutrients on a regular basis.

Fertilize in-ground plants once a month by working in a handful of compost at the base of each plant and watering in with worm tea, or organic liquid fertilizer mixed in a watering can or sprayer according to package directions. For the best production, fertilize container plants once a week by watering with worm tea in a watering can or sprayer and liquid organic fertilizer according to package directions.

Now that you have the basics on what keeps warm-weather veggies happy, it is time get our hands dirty and plant four popular warm-weather veggies, tomatoes, peppers, cucumbers, and squash.

CaliKim's Quick Tip: Warm Soil

Warm-weather veggies love warm soil and get off to a quick start when planted in soil that is 60°F (15°C) or warmer (usually a few weeks after the last frost date). Impatient to get your warm-weather seedlings in the ground? Cover your garden bed with black plastic a few weeks prior to planting. The sun will warm the soil faster through the plastic and you can get your seedlings planted sooner.

TOMATOES: THE CROWN JEWEL OF THE GARDEN

CaliKim's Quick Tip: Pruning Tomatoes

Tomatoes are notoriously prone to disease, which spreads quicker on leaves that get wet and don't dry off. Prune off branches from the bottom 6 to 12 inches (15 to 30 cm) of your tomato plant as it grows to allow for better air circulation. Also prune any yellowing or spotted leaves (signs of disease) as soon as they appear to keep plants healthier and stop the spread of disease.

Tomatoes are one of the most popular warm-weather, sun-loving vegetables. I consider them the crown jewel of the garden. I love everything about tomatoes—from the scent of the leafy plants to the gigantic heirloom tomatoes or the small cherry varieties dangling like sweet little suns from the vines. The flavor of a fresh, home-grown tomato is unmistakable. With a few simple tips, you're going to grow pounds and pounds of your own crown jewels.

When the weather is warm enough to grow tomatoes outdoors, plant tomato seedlings you started from seed indoors or transplants purchased from a garden center. Starting from seed indoors saves a ton of money and allows you to choose tomatoes of all colors, shapes, and sizes.

Garden center transplants are usually limited to the classic varieties, but purchasing tomato transplants is a good option if you are starting late in the growing season.

Seeds can also be planted directly in the garden (called "direct seeding"), but it's more difficult. Germination is much slower outside than when starting from seed indoors, as the soil needs to be warm and the seedlings need to be protected in cold weather with some type of cover.

If you have limited garden space, grow tomatoes in a container. Dwarf varieties can be grown in a container as small as 5 gallons (19 L). Larger varieties should be grown in a 10- to 20-gallon (38 to 76 L) container for best production. Containers should always have holes for drainage. Fill your container with a high-quality organic potting mix and moisten the soil prior to planting. See the Resources section (page 154) for my favorite containers and potting mix.

How to Plant a Tomato: Three Simple Steps

Prepare your garden beds and add amendments prior to planting (see Chapter 5). The steps are the same for planting in garden beds and containers, except where noted.

STEP 1

Dig a hole twice as deep and wide as the pellet or starter container the seedling is in.

In garden beds: Add a handful of compost and ¼ cup (30 g) of worm castings (optional but recommended) to each hole.

In containers: Add ¼ cup (30 g) worm castings for 5-gallon (19 L) containers and ½ to 1 cup (60 to 120 g) for 10- to 20-gallon (38 to 76 L) containers. Mix it into the container soil.

STEP 2

Peel the netting off the peat pellet. For a seedling in a container, carefully turn the container upside down to remove the seedling, grasping the stem between two fingers as you do so.

Tomatoes will grow roots wherever the stem touches the soil, so place the tomato seedling deep into in the hole, roots side down, leaving only the top one-third of the plant above the ground, pinching off the lower leaves. More roots mean a healthy plant, sturdy enough to support lots of tomatoes and withstand strong winds.

STEP 3

Fill the hole with soil around the seedling. Add another handful of compost and/or worm castings as you fill the hole. Water with worm tea and/or an organic liquid fertilizer high in nitrogen until the ground is evenly moist (in garden beds) or water runs out the bottom (containers). Worm tea adds beneficial bacteria and microbes to the soil, helps with root development, and helps with the overall health of the plant, protecting it from disease and pests. See Resources (page 154) for my favorite worm tea and fertilizer.

Give Tomatoes Their Space

If you want lots of tomatoes, give them lots of space. Plant each seedling 2 to 3 feet (60 to 90 cm) apart in the garden, or one seedling per container. They are large plants and need plenty of room to grow and absorb nutrients, but they also need airflow to keep them healthy. If tomatoes are planted too close together, the leaves won't have the air they need to dry off when they get wet. Wet leaves make the plant more prone to disease.

Support Your Tomatoes

Tomatoes are vining plants and need support so they don't sprawl all over your garden. Supporting them with a cage, stake, or sturdy trellis keeps them off the ground and saves space. It also gives them plenty of airflow, helping them be healthier so diseases and pests stay away.

DIY Tomato Cages

The most popular method of supporting tomatoes is a tomato cage—a wire enclosure that encircles your tomato plant and supports it as it grows. Cages are best installed at time of planting. Don't use the tomato cages from the garden center; they are not tall or strong enough to support a full-sized tomato plant, which can grow 8 to 10 feet (2.4 to 3 m) tall.

Sturdy DIY tomato cages are easy and inexpensive to make from rolls of 5-foot (1.5 m) wire fencing. Cut the roll of wire fencing into 5-foot (1.5 m) lengths and attach the sides of each with several zip ties or wire to form a tall circular cage.

Place the cage over your tomato seedlings at planting time, pushing the bottom of the cage into the soil around the plant. Weave a piece of rebar through the wire sections of each cage and drive it a foot (30 cm) into the ground or container soil for extra support near harvest. Depending on the size of the wire sections, you may need to cut out holes in the fencing so the tomatoes can fit through the wire when

harvested. DIY tomato cages last for years and make for easy garden maintenance, as the tomato plant does not need tying up as it grows.

Staking

Another method to support a tomato plant is with a tall, sturdy stake or pole. The pole should be 4 to 10 feet (1.2 to 3 m) tall, depending on the variety of tomato. Drive the pole 10 to 12 inches (26 to 30 cm) into the soil near the tomato at the time of planting. Get creative: Reuse what you already have for stakes. Tree branches, broom handles, or dried sunflower stalks are fun options.

The upside of staking is that it takes less space than a tomato cage. It is also super quick to install. The downside is that it requires more maintenance than cages: The tomato plant will need to be tied to the pole as it grows, and it will need to be pruned so it does not become too large for the pole to support.

I always love the day the first tomato seedling of the season is planted outside. It's a sure sign that summer is just around the corner. Tomatoes are easy to plant and grow. With a little TLC, in about 90 days they'll reward you with huge harvests. As you are eating one of nature's tastiest garden snacks, you'll feel a thrill of delight that you planted, nurtured, and grew it yourself.

PEPPERS: ALL COLORS, SHAPES, AND SIZES

Peppers are a warm-weather, sun-loving vegetable. They range from fiery hot to sweet and crunchy, and they are ornamental as well as edible. Pepper lovers, you've been waiting to plant your seedlings outside ever since you started seeds indoors a few months ago. Soon, you'll be seeing peppers of all colors, shapes, and sizes in your garden, and you'll be enjoying the amazing flavor of fresh peppers on your dinner plate.

When planting peppers, start seeds indoors and grow your own transplants, or purchase seedlings from a local garden center. They are very difficult to grow when direct seeded in the garden and will grow faster when started from seed in a warm and protected indoor environment. You'll save money when you grow your own transplants, and you can choose from unique varieties that will make your garden pop with color. Transplant selection at garden centers is usually limited to the classic varieties, but it is a good option if you are starting late in the growing season.

Peppers grow beautifully in containers as well as in garden beds. Grow one to two pepper plants in a 5-gallon (19 L) container, or three to four plants in a 10- to 20-gallon (38 to 76 L) container. Containers should always have holes for drainage. Fill your container with a high-quality organic potting mix. See the Resources section (page 154) for my favorite. Moisten the soil prior to planting.

CaliKim's Quick Tip: Pepper Germination

Pepper seeds can take 7 to 21 days to germinate and love to be warm and toasty. When starting from seed indoors, place the seedling tray on a heat mat (see Resources section, page 154). The seeds need bottom heat to germinate, and a heat mat will raise the temperature of the soil a few degrees and help the seeds sprout quicker.

How to Plant Peppers: Three Simple Steps

Prepare your garden beds prior to planting (see Chapter 5). The steps are the same for planting in garden beds and containers, except where noted.

STEP 1
Dig a hole a little deeper and wider than the pellet or starter container the seedling is in.

In garden beds: Add a handful of compost and ¼ cup (30 g) of worm castings (optional) to each planting hole.

In containers: Add ¼ cup (30 g) of worm castings for 5-gallon (19 L) containers and ½ to 1 cup (60 to 120 g) of worm castings for 10- to 20-gallon (38 to 76 L) containers. Mix it into the potting soil.

STEP 2

Peel the netting off the peat pellet. For a seedling in a starter container, carefully turn the container upside down, squeezing gently to remove the seedling, grasping the stem between two fingers as you do so. Place the seedling in the hole, roots down. The topsoil level of the seedling should be even with the surface of the hole. Fill the hole with soil around the seedling. Add another handful of compost (garden) or worm castings (containers) as you fill the hole.

STEP 3

Water with worm tea and/or an organic liquid fertilizer high in nitrogen until the ground is evenly moist (in garden beds) or until water runs out the bottom (containers). Worm tea adds beneficial bacteria and microbes to the soil and helps with root development. It also helps with the overall health of the plant, protecting it from disease and pests. Nitrogen encourages green, leafy growth so the plant is strong enough to produce lots of peppers.

Spacing for Peppers

Peppers grow to a height of 1 to 3 feet (30 to 90 cm). Space them 1 to 2 feet (30 to 60 cm) apart in garden beds. If you live in a climate with frequent temperatures over 95°F (35°C), plant them closer, 8 to 12 inches (20 to 30 cm) apart. This helps the plants shade each other, protecting the peppers from sun scald, a scarring and thinning of the skin from too much heat and sun exposure. Sun scald doesn't make a pepper inedible (the scalded part can be cut off), but it does affect its beauty. When growing in containers, grow one to two plants in a 5-gallon (19 L) container or three to four plants in a 10- to 20-gallon (38 to 76 L) container.

Support for Peppers

Pepper plants need support from a sturdy stake or small tomato cage to keep them from falling over when they are loaded down with peppers.

Make your own DIY cage or purchase 3-foot-tall (90 cm) tomato cages at the garden center, which are too small for tomatoes but work perfectly for peppers. Place the cage over the pepper seedling at planting time. Maintenance is easy, as the pepper will be supported by the cage as it grows. No tying up is needed.

To support with a stake, purchase a 4-foot (1.2 m) stake at the garden center or upcycle an old shovel handle or tree branch. Drive the stake in the soil near the base of the seedling at planting time. Tie the pepper stem to the stake as it grows.

You'll love seeing the rainbow of colors fully loaded pepper plants bring to the garden. Crazy as it sounds, sometimes I don't want to pick my peppers; I want to look at them and enjoy their beauty. However, we all know the real reward comes a few months after planting when you bring the pepper harvest brimming with freshness, color, and flavor in the house and eat your tasty treats for dinner.

For my video tutorial on how to grow peppers, please visit calikimgardenandhome.com/gardeningvideos.

PRO PEPPER TIP: OVERWINTERING

An established pepper plant can overwinter in a temperate climate. When pruned down to one *Y* branch and mulched with 2 to 3 inches (5 to 7.5 cm) of shredded leaves or straw, it will tolerate light frosts. The plant may not produce in cold temperatures, but it usually will survive and put out new growth (and new peppers) when the weather warms up.

CUCUMBERS: COOL, CRISP, AND SUMMERY

Slicing up a cool, crisp cucumber fresh off the vine is a summer must for gardeners. Are you a fan of the long, thin-skinned slicing cucumbers, ideal for fresh eating? Or do you love the shorter, spiny-skinned pickling cukes, perfect for making big jars of pickles? Whatever your preference, you will enjoy growing cucumbers in your garden and love eating them even more.

You have three options when planting cucumbers: Grow your own transplants from seeds started indoors and plant them outside as the weather warms up, plant seeds directly in your garden, or plant purchased transplants from the garden center. Cucumbers are easy to grow from seed, so I like to start seeds indoors as well as

CaliKim's Quick Tip: Stress-Free Cukes

If you have lots of summer days over 90°F (32°C) where you live, plant cukes where they get morning sun and afternoon shade to prevent them from overheating and getting stressed. If you don't have a spot in your garden with afternoon shade, make your own shade, or use shade cloth that will let some sunlight through. Cover your cucumber trellis with an old sheet on hot afternoons or drive four stakes in the ground around the plant and clip the corners of the sheet to each stake to make a shade tent.

For my video tutorial on how to grow cucumbers that are sweet and not bitter, please visit calikimgardenandhome.com/gardeningvideos.

DON'T STRESS THE CUKES

Yes, just like us, cucumbers can get stressed out—especially in the heat. When they are stressed, they tend to turn bitter. To grow cukes that are sweet and crunchy and not bitter, follow these five tips to provide them with a stress-free environment:

- Plant when the temperature is warm, 65–85°F (18–30°C).
- Plant in warm soil, at least 60°F (15°C).
- Don't let them dry out. Water regularly, especially when flowering and fruiting.
- Fertilize throughout the growing season— once a month with compost and worm tea.
- Harvest young and harvest often. Oversized cukes are usually bitter.

Often bitterness is concentrated at the ends of the cuke. Cut off each end and many times the middle will taste sweet.

direct seed outside every few weeks. This spreads the harvests out during the growing season.

Cucumbers grow beautifully in containers. You'll want to provide a cage or trellis for support. Grow a compact cucumber variety in a 5-gallon (19 L) container, or one to two full-sized plants in a 10- to 20-gallon (38 to 76 L) container. Containers should always have holes for drainage. Fill your container with a high-quality organic potting mix. See the Resources section (page 154) for my favorite containers and potting mix. Moisten the soil prior to planting.

How to Plant a Cucumber Seedling: Three Simple Steps

Prepare your garden beds prior to planting (see Chapter 5). The steps are the same for planting in the ground and in containers, except where noted. Cucumber seeds germinate quickly, and plants grow fast. Sow cucumber seeds every few weeks during the summer to keep the harvest coming all summer long.

STEP 1
Dig a hole little deeper and wider than the pellet or starter container the seedling is in.

In garden beds: Add a handful of compost and ¼ cup (30 g) of worm castings (optional but recommended) to each hole.

In containers: Add ¼ cup (30 g) of worm castings for 5-gallon (19 L) containers and ½ to 1 cup (60 to 120 g) of worm castings for 10- to 20-gallon (38 to 76 L) containers. Mix it into the soil.

STEP 2
Peel the netting off the peat pellet. For a seedling in a starter container, carefully turn the container upside down and squeeze gently to loosen the seedling, grasping the stem between two fingers as you do so. Place the seedling in the hole, roots down. The topsoil level of the seedling should be

even with the surface of the hole. Fill the hole with soil around the seedling. Add another handful of compost and/or worm castings as you fill.

STEP 3
Water with worm tea and an organic liquid fertilizer high in nitrogen until the ground is evenly moist (in garden beds) or water runs out the bottom (containers). Most liquid fertilizers are concentrated and should be diluted in water; follow the directions on the bottle.

Planting Cucumber Seeds: Three Simple Steps

Plant cucumber seeds at the same time as your transplants so you have cucumber plants at different stages of growth and have a harvest all season long.

STEP 1

In garden beds: Mix in a handful of compost and ¼ cup (30 g) of worm castings (optional but recommended) in the soil.

In containers: Add ¼ cup (30 g) of worm castings for 5-gallon (19 L) containers and ½ to 1 cup (60 to 120 g) of worm castings for 10- to 20-gallon (38 to 76 L) containers. Mix it into the potting mix.

STEP 2

Poke a hole in the soil ½ inch (1 cm) deep, spacing each hole 8 to 12 inches (20 to 30 cm) apart. Drop two to three seeds in each hole. Cover the seeds lightly with soil.

STEP 3

Water with worm tea and an organic liquid fertilizer high in nitrogen until the ground is evenly moist (in garden beds) or water runs out the bottom (containers). Most liquid fertilizers are concentrated and should be diluted in water; follow the directions on the bottle.

Spacing for Cucumbers

Cucumber plants like plenty of airflow to help prevent them from getting diseases common to cucumbers, such as powdery mildew. Plant seeds and seedlings 8 to 12 inches (20 to 30 cm) apart at the base of a trellis (such as a DIY tomato cage) or 6- to 8-foot (1 to 3 m) stake. When the seedlings are about 4 inches (10 cm) tall, thin them by pulling out the smaller weaker seedlings so they are 10 to 12 inches (25 to 30 cm) apart at the base of your trellis. This will give them plenty of space to grow and produce loads of delicious cucumbers for you and your family to pick fresh from the garden.

Support

If you are growing vining varieties (as opposed to bush varieties), they can grow 4 to 6 feet (1.2 to 1.8 m) tall. The vines grow best with some support. Growing vertically not only saves space, it provides airflow to keep the vines healthier and away from pests. There are many ways to trellis cucumbers. My two favorite ways are with DIY cages or a teepee trellis. Don't be afraid to experiment and repurpose materials that you already have for trellising. Come up with your own unique ideas and have fun with it.

DIY Cages

These are made from a roll of 5-foot (1.5 m) wire fencing in the same way as the DIY tomato cages, only smaller—about 12 inches (30 cm) in diameter. Adjust the size depending on your garden space. Place the cage over the cucumber at the time of planting. Plant maintenance is simple: Guide the plant up the cage as it grows; the tendrils will grab onto the cage and no tying up is necessary.

Teepee Trellis

Three 6- to 8-foot (1.8 to 2.4 m) poles are wired together at the top and spread apart to form a triangle teepee shape. These are quick, simple, and inexpensive to make. They also look natural and blend in well with garden foliage when tree branches or bamboo poles are used. This method requires a bit more maintenance than cages, as cucumbers need to be tied to the trellis as they grow.

Take care of your cucumber plants, provide a stress-free growing space with plenty of TLC, and they will give back to you as they start to produce fresh, delectable cucumbers for you and those you love to enjoy.

SQUASH: THE POWER PRODUCER

Squash is one of the easiest garden vegetables you'll grow. It's easy as pie to start from seed indoors or direct seed right in your garden. I like to plant squash seeds in the soil along with my transplants, so I have plants at all stages of growth. As one plant finishes producing, there's another plant just starting to produce, spreading the harvest out over the growing season.

Planting squash seeds with your kids is a fantastic way to get them excited about growing their own food. Your kids will love the quick results; the seeds break through the soil in just a few days. An added benefit to having your kids in the garden with you is that they always eat more veggies when they grow their own.

Squash transplants can be purchased from a garden center, and that's a good option if you are already in the warm summer months and want to pump out the harvest as soon as possible. However, the varieties available at most garden centers are limited. Starting from seed allows you to grow fun varieties and saves you money.

Squash is a large vegetable, but it can still be grown in a container if the container is large enough to provide adequate room for roots to grow. I recommend at least a 20-gallon (76 L) container for best production. My favorite containers for large vegetables such as squash are

Smart Pot fabric containers (see Resources, page 154). The fabric is durable and long lasting, and it is aerated, which means water drains easily and the roots can air prune. Air pruning means that the roots don't become rootbound as they do in plastic containers. Instead, they self-prune when they reach the sides of the container. This allows them to form a fibrous root mass, able to take up air and nutrients they need to grow lots of veggies. Any containers you use should always have holes (or breathable fabric) for drainage. Fill the containers with a high-quality organic potting mix (see Resources, page 154). Moisten the soil prior to planting.

TYPES OF SQUASH

There are two types of squash: summer squash and winter squash. Many people think summer squash are grown in the summer and winter squash in the winter. However, both types grow during summer months. Their names come from when they are harvested and eaten.

Summer squash is harvested about two months after planting and produces tons of squash during the warm spring and summer months until the first frost in the fall. Both the skin and flesh of summer squash are soft and edible. It is harvested throughout the summer months and eaten soon after harvesting, hence its name. Popular varieties include zucchini, crookneck, and pattypan.

Winter squash is left on the vine longer to ripen and harvested 3 to 4 months after planting, in the fall or early winter. The skin and flesh are hard, which helps it store for several months during the winter. Popular varieties include butternut and spaghetti squash.

How to Plant a Squash Seedling: Three Simple Steps

Prepare your garden beds prior to planting (see Chapter 5). If you are growing squash in a container, plant in a 15-gallon (57 L) container or larger for best production. Fill the container with a high-quality organic potting mix (see the Resources section, page 154). Moisten the soil prior to planting. The steps are the same for planting in the ground and in containers, except where noted.

STEP 1

Dig a hole little deeper and wider than the pellet or starter container the seedling is in.

In garden beds: Add a handful of compost and ¼ cup (30 g) of worm castings (optional but recommended) to each hole.

In containers: Mix ¼ cup (30 g) of worm castings in potting mix for 5-gallon (19 L) containers, and ½ cup (60 g) of worm castings for 10- to 20-gallon (38 to 76 L) containers. Mix it into the soil.

STEP 2

Peel the netting off the peat pellet. For a seedling in a starter container, carefully turn the container upside down to remove the seedling, grasping the stem between two fingers as you do so. Place the seedling in the hole, roots down. The topsoil level of the seedling should be even with the surface of the hole. Fill the hole with soil around the seedling. Add another handful of compost or 1 to 2 tablespoons (8 to 15 g) of worm castings around the plant as you fill the hole.

STEP 3

Water with worm tea and an organic liquid fertilizer high in nitrogen until the ground is evenly moist (in garden beds) or until water runs out the bottom (containers). Most liquid fertilizers are concentrated and should be diluted in water; follow the directions on the bottle.

Planting Squash Seeds: Three Simple Steps

Prepare your garden beds prior to planting (see Chapter 5). Plant squash seeds at the same time as your transplants so you have plants at all stages of growth and have a harvest all season long. The steps are the same for planting in the ground and in containers, except where noted.

STEP 1

In garden beds: Mix in a handful of compost and ¼ cup (30 g) of worm castings (optional but recommended) to the planting area.

In containers: Mix ½ cup (60 g) of worm castings into premoistened potting mix in a 20-gallon (76 L) container.

STEP 2

In garden beds: Poke a hole in the soil 1 inch (2.5 cm) deep, spacing each hole 2 to 3 feet (60 to 90 cm) apart.

In containers: Poke a 1-inch (2.5 cm) hole in the potting mix, one hole per 20-gallon (76 L) container. Drop two to three seeds in each hole. This gives you backups in case one or more seeds do not germinate. Cover the seed lightly with soil.

STEP 3

Water with worm tea and an organic liquid fertilizer high in nitrogen until the ground is evenly moist (in garden beds) or until water runs out the bottom (containers). Most liquid fertilizers are concentrated and should be diluted in water; follow the directions on the bottle.

Give Them Space and Watch Them Grow!

Squash like an abundance of space. I'm always tempted to crowd my squash, so I can fit as many plants in as possible. However, I've found that the more space I give them, the more they are the power producers they are famous for. This also provides them with airflow around the plants and will help prevent powdery mildew.

Spacing for Vining Varieties: Grow Up, Not Out

To grow more squash in a small amount of space, grow vining winter squash varieties (e.g., butternut, spaghetti, acorn) vertically on a 6- to 8-foot tall (2 to 3 m) trellis, rather than letting them sprawl on the ground. Space transplants or seeds 2 to 3 feet (60 to 90 cm) apart and tie them to the trellis as they grow. This maximizes space and adds visual interest; the squash look beautiful hanging down from a trellis as they mature.

Don't spend a ton of money or get complicated with trellising. Keep it inexpensive and get creative with what you already have. Use DIY tomato cages, repurpose tree branches to create a teepee trellis, or reuse old fencing or a cattle panel. One of my viewers even used an old box spring for a trellis. Experiment with different items that will make your garden your own fun, unique space.

Spacing for Bush Varieties

Zucchini, pattypan, and crookneck squash are bush varieties that grow 3 to 4 feet (1 to 2 m) high and wide, and the leaves are quite large. Space transplants and seeds at least 3 feet (1 m) apart to give them plenty of space to produce loads of squash for you to pick fresh from the garden and bring straight to your table.

Enjoy growing and eating summer and winter squash. These power producers will reward your loving care many times over with delectable, fresh-from-the-garden food that will melt in your mouth. You'll be proud to share summer squash with many of your friends and family in the warm months, and you will have an abundance of winter squash to enjoy during the months when it's too cold to grow outside.

For my video tutorial on how to grow squash, please visit calikimgardenandhome.com/gardeningvideos.

TIPS FOR PURCHASING TRANSPLANTS—CHOOSE WINNERS NOT DUDS

Although starting from seed saves money and provides interesting varieties, the reality is sometimes you don't have the time or the space to grow your own seedlings and will purchase them from the local garden center. Follow these tips to save money, choose the winners, and avoid the duds:

- Look at the roots: They should nearly fill the container, and they should have loose, white, fibrous growth. Plants with roots that are circling around the container (rootbound) have been in the container too long and are not the best choice.
- Look at the leaves: Choose plants with healthy, green leaves with even color and without spots to minimize the risk of introducing disease into your garden.
- Look under the leaves: This is a favorite hiding spot for garden pests. Choose plants that are pest-free for a healthy garden.
- Look for buds not flowers: Select plants that have buds rather than flowers to minimize flower drop, which will slow down vegetable production.
- Look at the soil: Choose seedlings with evenly moist soil. Super dry or waterlogged soil may cause seedlings to be stressed and stunted.

Be sure to plant purchased seedlings within 2 to 3 days for the best chance of success.

COOL-WEATHER VEGETABLES

Fall or early spring days are perfect for growing cool-weather veggies such as lettuce, peas, radishes, cabbage, beets, celery, broccoli, cauliflower, carrots, and all kinds of greens.

When to Plant Cool-Weather Veggies Outdoors

Cool-weather veggies can be planted outdoors a few weeks before the last frost date in the early spring or in the cooler days of fall. In a temperate winter climate, such as where I live in Southern California, the best time to grow cool-weather veggies is in the winter.

Cool-weather veggies thrive in daytime temperatures under 75°F (23°C). Many cool-weather veggies are frost tolerant and will survive cold nights with light frosts (32°F/0°C), especially if the plants are growing in the ground and well established before frost hits. Cool-weather veggies do not tolerate heat well. They may turn bitter in temperatures over 80°F (27°C). They may also shoot up a tall stalk from the center of the plant ("bolt"), and develop flowers, then seeds—nature's way of producing the next generation

of plants. To help prevent bolting, provide cool-weather veggies with some shade during hot weather (over 80°F/27°C) with four stakes and an old sheet draped over the stakes/plants.

Sunlight Needs for Cool-Weather Veggies

As long as they are planted in temperatures under 75°F (23°C), cool-weather veggies are sun lovers. Plant them where they get 6 to 8 hours of sun a day for the most production. Some (such as lettuce and greens), will still produce in 4 to 6 hours of sunlight a day. Planting cool-weather veggies where they get morning sun and afternoon shade will help them survive in temperatures over 75°F (23°C).

Now that you have a general idea of what keeps cool-weather veggies happy, let's get down and dirty with step-by-step planting details for two popular cool-weather veggies: lettuce and peas.

LETTUCE: THE GATEWAY VEGETABLE

If you have never grown anything before, lettuce is a perfect vegetable to start with. It is super easy to grow in a container or in the ground. And once you've grown lettuce and tasted sweet success, you'll find other vegetables are not so intimidating to grow. Kids love planting lettuce because they enjoy the immediate satisfaction of seeing seeds break through the soil in just a few days. Help them plant lettuce in their own container or plot of lettuce. You might be surprised at how much more they gobble up salads they grow themselves.

Lettuce can be started in peat pellets or containers inside and then planted outside when the temperature is 75°F (23°C) or under. However, the easiest way to grow lettuce is to plant seeds directly in your garden beds or containers. Choose a container that is at least 6 inches (15 cm) deep and a foot or so (30 cm) in diameter. Fill the container with potting mix. See the Resources section (page 154) for my favorites. Moisten the soil prior to planting.

How to Plant Lettuce: Three Simple Steps

Prepare your garden beds prior to planting (see Chapter 5). The steps are the same for planting in the ground and in containers, except where noted.

STEP 1

In the garden: Mix an inch (2.5 cm) of compost into the planting area (make your own or purchase bagged at garden center). Add worm castings (optional, but recommended), loosening the soil with a pitchfork or shovel as you mix in soil amendments.

In a container: Mix in ¼ cup (30 g) of worm castings into the potting mix.

CaliKim's Quick Tips: Growing Lettuce

Plant a container or two of lettuce just outside your kitchen door so you can step outside and pick what you need for a fresh salad in minutes.

Move your container to the shade or inside during hot weather to help it keep producing in the heat.

To delay bolting, provide your lettuce plants with some shade during hot weather (over 80°F/27°C) with four stakes and an old sheet. Or, plant your lettuce at the base of taller veggies, such as tomatoes or cucumbers.

Plant additional seeds every 2 weeks to keep the harvests coming.

STEP 2

Sprinkle seeds lightly on the surface of the soil in rows, spacing rows 6 to 12 inches (15 to 30 cm) apart, or sprinkle in a circular pattern for a round container. Don't worry too much about seed spacing as seedlings can be thinned as they grow. Cover seeds very lightly with soil; they are tiny and may not germinate if they are covered heavily.

STEP 3

Water with worm tea and an organic liquid fertilizer high in nitrogen until the ground is evenly moist (in garden beds) or until water runs out the bottom (containers). Most liquid fertilizers are concentrated and should be diluted in water; follow the directions on the bottle.

Plant lettuce seeds today and you'll be eating a homegrown salad in about a month. Growing your own fresh supply of leafy greens means you'll save money at the grocery store and you'll have the wonderful experience of stepping into your backyard to pick your own nutritious salads.

For my video tutorial on how to grow lettuce, please visit calikimgardenandhome.com/gardeningvideos.

PEAS: THE PERFECT GARDEN SNACK

It's almost impossible to grow too many peas in my garden. They are sweet and tasty; peas are the perfect garden snack. In fact, very few make it into the house. Peas are one of the first cool-weather veggies you can plant outside, are super quick to grow, and go from seed to your table in 6 to 8 weeks, ideal for the impatient gardener.

Pea seeds can be started inside in peat pellets or containers 4 weeks before the first frost date of the fall or last frost date of the spring. Then plant them in the garden when the temperature is 75°F (23°C) or under. However, the easiest way to grow peas is to plant seeds directly in your garden beds or containers.

For container growing, choose a container that is at least 2 feet (60 cm) deep and at least 1 to 2 feet (30 to 60 cm) in diameter; a 10-gallon (38 L) container is perfect. Fill the container with potting mix. Moisten the soil prior to planting.

How to Plant Peas: Three Simple Steps

Prepare your garden beds prior to planting (see Chapter 5). Plant pea seeds outside at the same time you plant pea seedlings (started indoors) in the garden. This way you have plants at all stages of growth and have a harvest all season long. The steps are the same for planting in the ground and in containers, except where noted.

STEP 1
In the garden: Mix an inch (2.5 cm) of compost into the planting area (make your own or purchase bagged at garden center). Add worm castings (optional, but recommended), loosening the soil with a pitchfork or shovel as you mix in soil amendments.

In a container: Mix in ½ cup (60 g) of worm castings for a 10-gallon (38 L) container into the potting mix.

STEP 2

Poke a hole in the soil ½ inch (1 cm) deep. Drop two to three seeds in each hole. Cover the seeds with soil.

STEP 3

Water with worm tea and an organic liquid fertilizer high in nitrogen until the ground is evenly moist (in garden beds) or until water runs out the bottom (containers). Most liquid fertilizers are concentrated and should be diluted in water; follow the directions on the bottle.

Spacing and Support for Peas

Many pea varieties are vining plants and need a trellis. Plant pea seeds and seedlings 4 to 6 inches (10 to 15 cm) apart at the base of a teepee trellis, DIY cage, 5- to 6-foot (1.5 to 1.8 m) stake, or large store-bought tomato cage. The plants may need guiding up the trellis, but the tendrils will naturally grab on to the trellis and climb up as they grow.

For my video tutorial on how to grow peas, please visit calikimgardenandhome.com/gardeningvideos.

Planting Your Garden Grocery Store

To plant your own garden grocery store, all you need to do is follow the simple tips and tricks from this chapter. With just a little practice, you'll learn the simple skills you need to grow your own food. You'll have joy in your heart seeing the seeds you lovingly planted and tended grow into organic vegetables that you'll soon be harvesting, eating, and sharing with friends and family.

Along with the good times, as your garden grows, the challenges *will* come. Expect it and you won't be as discouraged when the tough times visit your garden. However, don't panic. In the next chapter, I'll share practical tips to handle the challenges so they don't get the best of you.

CaliKim's Quick Tips: Peas

If you time it right, you can have two crops of mouthwatering peas each year. The secret is to plant them at the right time: as early as possible in the spring, two weeks before your last frost date. Then, later in the season, plant a fall crop. For a fall crop, plant them 8 to 10 weeks before your first frost date, and you'll have peas to eat going into winter. In mild winter climates, grow peas during the cooler winter months and you'll be eating delectable peas on your winter salads.

To maximize garden space, tuck peas in (with a pole for support) wherever you have an empty spot in your garden—in between radishes, spinach, lettuce, or other greens.

Kids love to plant peas as seeds are large and easy to handle. The seeds will germinate in a few days. Kids will love to help you start seeds inside in paper cups, watch them grow daily, and plant them outside when the weather is right.

8

GARDEN CHALLENGES—PEST AND DISEASE CONTROL, EXTREME WEATHER

I WAS HORRIFIED. I stared in dismay at my prized tomato plant. Just the day before, it had three gorgeous, orange, juicy beefsteak tomatoes ready for the picking. Now my precious gems were a shredded mess. I felt like crying. Three months of hard work down the drain in one fell swoop, the victim of a rodent's nighttime forage through my backyard.

Don't you wish we could grow our veggies in a dream garden with the perfect soil and disease-free plants, where there are no weeds, pests, pesky critters, or extreme weather? If you find this paradise, kindly give me a heads up, will you? I'll be there in a flash with a million different seeds to plant.

The experience of growing your own food is spectacular and provides a one-of-a-kind satisfaction. But let's keep it real. Growing a garden has its challenges right along with the high points.

Each growing season has a different set of woes. One summer I picked countless dreaded tomato hornworms off my tomato plants. The next year the cabbage loopers decimated my kale. Another growing season brought extreme heat and drought, and the spider mites attacked with a vengeance. The same summer the rodents quenched their thirst by systematically hollowing out my cantaloupe and watermelon each night.

When we see the veggies we worked months to grow destroyed by something beyond our control, it's disheartening. To be honest, some days I've wondered if it was worth the effort to grow my own veggies. There were a few times I even felt like giving up.

As discouraging as the lows are, take heart. In this chapter, I share simple, natural, organic methods, free from synthetic pesticides, to prevent and combat weeds, pests, and diseases before they get out of hand. This chapter gives you a plan to deal with the lows. There are also easy ways to protect your garden from unexpected frosts or to extend your growing season when winter comes early or stays late. And let's not forget about how to protect your precious veggies from burning up in the extreme summer heat.

Finding solutions that work for you is part of what makes gardening a fun adventure. The reward of bringing in a heaping harvest basket will renew your spirit and make it all worthwhile, despite the challenges that come your way.

This chapter is not designed to be a comprehensive guide to every single pest, plant disease, or weed you might encounter in your garden. It will, however, give you some tips to have up your sleeve for preventing setbacks before they happen. It will arm you with tips for controlling pests and diseases organically when they do rear their ugly heads. It will also provide simple ways you can make the best of crazy weather while having a fun, positive attitude along the way!

PREVENTION IS THE BEST CURE

Prevention is always the best cure. Once you get a pest infestation or disease sets, in it's always harder to control. Be proactive. Don't wait until it's too late. The best defense is a good offense.

Tip 1: Check Your Garden Daily

One of the best ways you can launch your offense is to check your garden daily. Always be aware of what's going on in the nooks and crannies of your garden beds and containers. Take a few moments each morning or evening to stroll through the garden and check on your plants. I like to do this in the morning with a cup of coffee; there's nothing like starting the day with a dose of garden therapy. It is relaxing and enjoyable, and it gives you the chance to stop a problem in its tracks, before it gets out of hand.

Tip 2: Healthy Soil and Plants

Steer clear of garden challenges right up front by building healthy soil. Healthy soil often results in healthy plants. Healthy plants will be less attractive to pests, and the plants won't be as stressed if the weather goes rogue on you. Soil rich in organic matter will be more likely to grow sturdy plants that are able to bounce back when a critter decides to eat half the plant for a night-time snack.

How do you build healthy soil? Add organic matter on a regular basis to improve your soil over time. Keep costs down by collecting and shredding leaves in the fall and making your own compost. Add your shredded leaves, compost, and purchased worm castings to your garden beds at the start of each growing season, and once a month throughout. Compost and worm castings feed your soil powerful, organic nutrients, and they add beneficial bacteria and microbes. These tiny organisms settle in around the roots of your plants, fighting off the bad soil-dwelling organisms, keeping your plants healthy and less vulnerable to pests and diseases. Shredded leaves will break down in the soil over time and help it retain water and bring in the worms like crazy. Worms aerate the soil, making it easier for the roots to breathe and grow into healthy, strong plants.

Tip 3: Barriers

Protect your plants at the time of planting with a barrier. Row covers made from shade cloth, or old sheer curtains secured with clips to stakes and draped over garden beds, work well to protect plants from cabbage moths, caterpillars, or critters. Make sure the material is sheer and breathable to allow for sunlight and airflow.

Place empty paper towel rolls (cut in thirds) or water bottles (cut in half with the bottom and tops cut out) as barriers around stems of transplants. This will help protect against chewing insects, such as slugs and snails, that might be on the prowl for young tender seedlings.

Tip 4: Companion Planting

Another organic method to cut down on the pest population is to plant flowers and plants that will attract pollinators and beneficial insects, such as ladybugs and praying mantises, that are natural predators of the bad bugs. Cosmos, milkweed, wildflowers, yarrow, borage, poppies, bachelor's buttons, sunflowers, and nasturtiums—to name just a few—are terrific beneficial insect attractors. Some flowers and herbs such as marigolds and dill give off an odor that many pests do not like and will send them packing. Hot pepper plants and garlic may discourage certain pests from biting into plants around them.

GO ON THE DEFENSE

Expect it. Despite your best efforts, sometimes pests and diseases will attack. Don't get discouraged and quit. Instead, have a plan. A few organic defensive tools in your back pocket will go a long way toward stopping issues. You'll be ready to knock 'em down before the problem gets out of control.

There are many quick, simple, and inexpensive organic tips for pest and disease control, but keep in mind they aren't "one and done." Organic methods need to be applied consistently to be effective. It might be quicker to grab a chemical pesticide spray from the garden center, but resist the urge. When you pick that homegrown, organic tomato off the vine, you'll have peace of mind knowing that it's the healthiest, freshest, tastiest tomato possible—and it's chemical-free. You'll know exactly what went into growing it and feel proud to feed it to your family.

Tip 1: Water

The defense I use most often is so simple that I overlooked it for many years. It's as close as your garden hose. Water. A strong spray of water from your garden hose knocks many smaller, soft-bodied pests, such as aphids, earwigs, and spider mites, off your plants and sends them packing, sometimes for good.

THE FORMULA
Using a garden hose with a nozzle, spray the stems and leaves (tops and bottoms) with water. Rub the leaves as you spray to knock the bugs off.

HOW OFTEN TO SPRAY
Spray at the first sign of pests on your plants. Check 24 hours later. If the bugs hang around, spray again. Spray every 1 to 2 weeks for prevention.

Tip 5: Stop the Weeds in Their Tracks

Raise your hand if you love spending hours weeding your garden. What, no hands up? Want to know my best offense against weeds? One word: mulch. Spread several inches of shredded leaves, straw, or pine needles (or a combo of all three) on your garden beds and walkways. This helps your garden retain moisture, and it smothers out weeds. When the weeds do grow, the soil is softer, making them easier to remove.

Along with mulch on the top of your garden beds, lay down thick cardboard as a weed barrier on the bottom of raised beds and walkways. Then fill your beds with soil, lay down several inches of wood chips on your walkways, and you are good to go. All but the most persistent weeds will be out of sight, out of light, and out of mind.

Empty soil is an invitation for weeds to run rampant, and they certainly don't need a second invitation. Plant densely to shade out weeds and cut down on a gardener's most dreaded task.

When the weeds do pop up, pull them right away, long before they go to seed and spread. Check your garden daily and stay on top of the weeds before they become a problem.

Tip 2: Soap and Water

My second line of defense against pests is a simple soap-and-water spray. This can be effective on soft-bodied insects, such as aphids, spider mites, whiteflies, earwigs, and cabbage loopers. Use a natural dish soap—such as castile dish soap—not hand soap. Always choose a soap without additives or degreasers; these could harm your plants.

THE FORMULA

Measure 2 to 4 tablespoons (15 to 60 ml) natural dish soap into a gallon jug of water. Shake and pour in a spray bottle or pump sprayer. This spray will keep indefinitely.

HOW OFTEN TO SPRAY

Spray at the first sign of pests on your plants. Check 24 hours later. If the bugs are still there, spray again.

Tip 3: Neem Oil and Peppermint Oil

Different sprays will work in different growing conditions. If the pests aren't deterred with the soapy oil spray, use neem oil and peppermint oil as a third line of defense. Oils smother soft-bodied, chewing, and sucking insects, such as aphids, cabbage loopers, earwigs, and slugs.

Neem oil is organic and comes from the neem tree. Besides smothering the soft-bodied insects, it also disrupts their life cycle. In order for neem oil to be effective, it should be 100-percent virgin, cold pressed, with azadirachtin (see Resources, page 154). Azadirachtin is a component derived from the seed kernels of the neem tree that disrupts the insect's life cycle. Neem oil without azadirachtin will not be effective.

CaliKim's Quick Tip: Garden Sprays

Any sprays should be applied in the cool of the day, not in direct sunlight. Morning is preferable as it allows plants to dry during the day. The effectiveness of sprays will vary according to type of plant, climate, weather conditions, and sunlight exposure. Start with the minimal recommended amount of a soap- or oil-based product. Work your way up to the maximum recommend amount, but only if the problem continues.

Always, always, always test spray a few affected leaves first. Wait 48 hours to see how your plant responds; different soaps and oils will work differently. If there is damage, such as burned spots, leaves curling, or discoloration, adjust the amount of product you're using and test spray again. If there are no negative effects on the plant, spray the entire plant, including the stem and leaves (undersides and tops) until the plant is dripping wet. If the pest issue continues, work your way up to a larger amount of product, always test spraying when you make any changes. Never exceed the rates provided by the manufacturer on the label if you're using a commercial brand.

Neem oil is safe for bees and beneficial insects if it is not sprayed on them directly. Mix with water and spray on the leaves early in the morning so it dries on the leaves quickly. When the chewing insects munch on the leaves coated in neem oil, it disrupts their gut and their ability to reproduce. The bees and beneficial insects won't be harmed because they don't chew the plants. Take care not to spray bees directly, and don't spray flowers directly where bees and beneficial insects will be feeding.

Peppermint oil is a natural pest repellent (see Resources, page 154). It may help mask the scent of your plants, so insects are deterred from having a feeding fest. These two oils can be used in combination or used separately.

THE FORMULA

Measure 1 to 2 tablespoons (15 to 30 ml) neem oil and ½ to 1 teaspoon (5 to 10 ml) peppermint oil in 1 gallon (4 L) of water. Add 1 to 2 tablespoons (15 to 30 ml) of natural dish soap to disperse the oil throughout the water as you shake it. Pour in a spray bottle or pump sprayer. Test spray and wait 48 hours. If there is no damage to the plant, spray the entire infested area, shaking the bottle frequently.

Prune out yellow, discolored, and spotted leaves to prevent the disease from spreading. Do not compost diseased leaves because you don't want the diseases spreading to the rest of your garden through your compost. To help avoid common tomato diseases, such as blight, prune the stems and leaves off the bottom 6 to 12 inches (15 to 30 cm) of the plant to provide airflow. You should also keep the leaves as dry as possible.

Powdery mildew is a fungal disease that commonly affects squash and cucumbers. You'll know when you have powdery mildew in your garden because your squash plant looks like someone sprinkled baby powder on the leaves. The powdery-like spots spread rapidly. Prune off affected leaves at the first sign of spots and use a simple milk-and-water spray to help prevent it and keep it under control. The protein in the milk has an antiseptic effect on leaves when sprayed in direct sunlight and helps control the powdery mildew fungus.

THE FORMULA

Mix 1 part milk to 3 parts water. I used cow's milk; whole or skim is fine. Pour the solution in a spray bottle or pump sprayer. Spray in direct sunlight. Test spray on a few leaves and wait 48 hours. If there is no damage to the plant, spray the entire plant.

HOW OFTEN TO SPRAY

Spray every 1 to 2 weeks for prevention. Spray every 3 to 5 days when powdery mildew is affecting your plant.

For my video tutorial on how to use milk spray to control powdery mildew, please visit calikimgardenandhome.com/gardeningvideos.

HOW OFTEN TO SPRAY

Spray every 5 to 7 days (3 to 4 cycles) to give the neem oil a chance to kill the entire life cycle of the insects. This is not a one-and-done solution; you'll need to spray on a regular basis to be effective. Spray every 1 to 2 weeks for prevention.

For my video tutorial on how to use neem oil and peppermint oil in the garden, please visit calikimgardenandhome.com/gardeningvideos.

Tip 4: Prune Diseased Leaves and Use Milk Spray for Powdery Mildew

It's inevitable that plant diseases will rear their ugly heads in your garden at some point in the growing season. Diseases are more likely to attack and spread during times of high humidity and when plant leaves get wet and stay wet. Give your plants the best chance of staving off common tomato diseases and powdery mildew. Water at the bottom of your plants and use any garden sprays in the morning so that plants have time to dry during the day.

WEATHER CHALLENGES

Okay, the bad news first: No matter how hard we try, we can't control the weather—so don't stress about it! The good news: We can do a few simple things to extend the growing season or protect our veggies in the cold or heat. As a rule, work with the weather, not against it, by planting the right veggies in the right season. But when a late frost threatens your newly planted tomato plant or an unexpected heat wave threatens to boil your tomatoes on the vine, here are a few tips and tricks to use.

Cold Weather

Protect plants from unexpected frosts or cold nights with DIY winter covers. To cover small plants, use a plastic storage bin or gallon jug with the bottom cut out. For larger areas, put stakes in the ground around the garden beds, then drape a thick blanket or large piece of plastic over your plants. Remove covers when the sun comes up; it will heat up quickly under the covers and plants may get overheated. Simple winter covers are also a great way to extend the growing season in the fall or get an early start in the spring.

For my video tutorial on how to make an easy DIY winter cover, please visit calikimgardenandhome.com/gardeningvideos.

Hot Weather

Most veggies get stressed and won't produce well in temperatures over 90°F (32°C). To protect your garden during hot spells, make sure it is well fed. An extra feeding of compost, worm castings, and worm tea helps them manage the heat stress. Check daily, sometimes twice daily, during extreme heat to make sure your garden is hydrated. Using stakes in the ground and draping shade cloth over your plants can go a long way toward protecting them from intense heat. Shade cloth is a mesh cloth that allows for airflow but blocks out a percentage of the sun's rays. I've found that a 40 precent sun block shade cloth works well during high temperatures to protect my veggies (see Resources, page 154).

For my video tutorial on how to protect your garden during a heat wave, please visit calikimgardenandhome.com/gardeningvideos.

Don't Give Up!

One of the most important things you can do to keep a good attitude is to deal with the challenges and don't put all your eggs in one basket. Always plant backups to account for plants that will be lost to pests, disease, or weather. When you have extra plants, you won't be as discouraged when one plant dies, because you will have another waiting in the wings to take its place.

You might be tempted to call it quits when garden struggles come your way. But remember, I'm right there with you. I want to encourage you—don't give up! Many gardeners give up early and miss out on the joys and rewards of gardening. To experience the highs, you'll have to go through some lows. Expect it and you won't be as discouraged when the tough times come. In the end, it's all worth it. Bringing in a dazzling haul of wholesome, organic veggies fresh from the garden to the dinner table feels like a million bucks. Knowing that you've grown them yourself and can now share them with your loved ones is a one-of-a-kind satisfaction that brings rewards to your life that go far beyond eating veggies. That experience is well worth any challenges that you overcome.

9

HARVESTING ORGANIC VEGETABLES LIKE A PRO

"WHAT IF I DO SOMETHING TO MESS IT UP?"

I'd worked for months planting, nurturing, and checking on my garden daily, protecting it from pests and diseases. I watched over my tomatoes, peppers, squash, and cucumbers as if they were my precious babies, and I was overjoyed that harvest day was getting closer. I had been dreaming for months about putting the first plate of garden-fresh, organic vegetables on the table for my family. I imagined how I would feel. Satisfied. Proud. Like I had accomplished something important.

But I was scared. As a newbie gardener, I didn't have a clue how to harvest a tomato, let alone any of the other vegetables I was growing. What if I picked my squash before it was ripe, and it was small and flavorless? What if I waited too long to harvest my prized tomatoes, and they were overripe and mushy? And once I picked my beautiful peppers, how should I store them until we could eat them all? What if I ruined my hard work by one lousy mistake?

Can you relate? Do you have the same dreams, doubts, and fears I did about when to pick your prized organic vegetables? Have you ever wondered if those stunning harvest baskets you see on Instagram and YouTube videos are from a real garden? If so, I'm guessing you might be certain you won't be the one bringing in picture-perfect harvest baskets anytime soon. Or will you?

HARVEST DAY

This is why we gardeners do it. Harvesting is the ultimate reward for your hard work. The garden gives back with fresh vegetables from your own organic grocery store.

Learning how to harvest your vegetables— and learning simple ways to prepare and store them—isn't as daunting as you may think. I found that with a little practice and some harvesting tips and tricks, I was soon picking fresh veggies like a seasoned pro. And you will too.

In this chapter, you'll find detailed harvesting tips for the most popular warm- and cool-weather vegetables to help you bring in your veggies at the

peak of ripeness, full of freshness and flavor. You'll also find storage tips for your harvest, along with quick tips for many other vegetables you might grow in your garden. Once you master the harvesting basics, you'll be showing off your stunning harvest baskets with the confidence of a seasoned pro and be making delicious garden-to-table meals that will delight your family and friends.

Not an Exact Science

One thing that might surprise you is that the "rules" for timing your harvest are not an exact science. Days from seed to harvest (also known as days to maturity) vary for each vegetable.

Temperature, the ideal amount of sunlight, and the health of each plant due to pests and diseases can also affect how long a vegetable takes to ripen. If the conditions are less than the best, days from seed to harvest may be longer.

Experiment, Experiment, Experiment

Gardening is not one size fits all. There are many ways to reach the goal of putting fresh, home-grown food on the table. Experiment to learn what size to pick your vegetables and harvest them at the size you like to eat them. Pick a few cucumbers "too soon," and you might find you love them small and tender. Wait "too long" to harvest zucchini until it's baseball bat–sized, and you might discover you enjoy large, sliced squash medallions in a veggie lasagna.

Follow the harvest advice in this chapter—but remember, these are general guidelines only. How will you ever find out what delights you the most if you don't break the rules occasionally? Give yourself permission to have less-than-flawless veggies. Your garden should reflect *you*, your tastes, your personality, and your preferences.

Keep the Harvests Coming

Our goal as gardeners is to keep the harvests coming so we always have fresh and tasty food to eat. For many vegetables, the more you harvest, the more they will produce. Harvesting redirects the plant's energy into producing new vegetables and allows them to grow multiple rounds. This way you can grow as many vegetables as possible over the growing season.

Leaving ripe veggies on the plant past their peak not only sends a signal to the plant to stop producing, it also encourages pests and rodents to attack. It's always frustrating to lose your precious garden treats to the critters.

Once your plants start growing tiny baby veggies, they'll grow by leaps and bounds. Make it habit to take a stroll through the garden each day to see if anything is ready to harvest. It will put a smile on your face, you'll pick what is ripe, and you will bring in a basket brimming with flavor and freshness.

HARVESTING TOMATOES: THE CROWN JEWEL OF THE GARDEN

A vine-ripened tomato harvested at its peak explodes with flavor. You'll crave more. And more. Once you grow your own, store-bought tomatoes will never satisfy you again.

When to Harvest Tomatoes

Tomatoes are ready to harvest 60 to 90 days after you transplant the seedlings outdoors, depending on the tomato variety and the weather conditions. Harvest the fruit when the color is true to the variety: red varieties are red, orange are orange, yellow are yellow. A tomato at its peak will give slightly to pressure when squeezed.

TWO TYPES OF TOMATOES

Determinate: On determinate tomatoes, the fruit is produced and ripens all at once, usually within a few weeks, and then the plant dies. These varieties give you large harvests all at once to preserve, can, or freeze.

Indeterminate: On indeterminate tomatoes, the fruit is produced and ripens all season long, and the plant will not die until the first frost in the fall (although you will see a noticeable decline in productivity as the weather cools off). These varieties give you a harvest over time that is easier to manage.

Quick and Simple Tomato Harvest Tips

- Leave your tomatoes on the vine as long as possible for the best flavor and color.

- An unripe tomato will be harder and lighter than a ripe tomato.

- Once you start harvesting your tomato crop, check daily for ripe tomatoes.

- Overripe tomatoes will rot quickly and bring in pests and rodents.

- Smaller, cherry-type tomatoes ripen sooner, about 60 days after planting.

- Harvest cherry tomatoes as soon as they are ripe as they crack easily.

- Larger, beefsteak-type tomatoes take longer to ripen, about 90 days after planting.

Tomato Storage and Eating Tips

Don't refrigerate tomatoes—it diminishes the garden-fresh flavor. Store tomatoes away from direct sunlight, in a basket or on the countertop. A sunny windowsill is not a good place. They may rot before you eat them.

An unripe tomato will continue to ripen off the vine. They produce ethylene gas, which encourages ripening. Ripen green tomatoes off the vine by placing them in a closed paper bag, a cardboard box lined with newspaper, or in a bag with a green banana. This keeps the ethylene gas contained in an enclosed space for faster ripening.

Homegrown tomatoes are unbelievably delicious sliced up and eaten fresh on a salad or in a sandwich. Pair them with basil for a tasty treat or chop them into fresh bruchetta or pico de gallo. Use your garden-fresh treats to make your own ketchup, marinara sauce, salsa, and bruchetta. The sky is the limit. Preserve your tomatoes for later use by canning up your favorite recipes, or wash them and pop them whole in a freezer bag and place in the freezer for later use in cooking.

How to Harvest a Tomato

Grasp the tomato in one hand and the stem in the other hand. Pull the tomato gently from the vine, leaving about ¼ inch (6 mm) of the stem on the tomato. If the tomato does not separate easily from the vine, use scissors to cut the tomato from the plant, leaving about ¼ inch (6 mm) of the stem on the tomato.

CaliKim's Top Tomato Picks

Kellogg's Breakfast: Large beefsteak variety, loaded with juice and sweetness. Delicious sliced on sandwiches or in fresh salsa.

Amish Paste: Giant, meaty Roma variety. Perfect for sauces and canning.

Yellow Brandywine: Heirloom with fuzzy potato leaf vines, produces up to 2 pounds (about 1 kg). Exceptional flavor and creamy texture.

Tiny Tim: Dwarf tomato, 1 to 2 feet (30 to 60 cm) tall, produces tons of cherry tomatoes. Good for containers, patios, and small gardens.

HARVESTING PEPPERS: FIERY HOT TO SWEET AND CRUNCHY

The rainbow shades of peppers are a stunning sight in your raised beds, containers, or tucked in small spots around your garden. I love seeing the beautiful array of colored peppers growing outside. Crazy as it sounds, sometimes I don't want to pick my peppers; I just want to look at them and enjoy their beauty.

You'll love stepping outside to pick your own fresh peppers. They are prolific producers. Get ready—your family and friends will rave about the recipes you make from your pepper crop.

When to Harvest Peppers

Peppers are ready to harvest 60 to 90 days after you transplant the seedling outdoors, depending on the variety and the weather conditions. You can harvest peppers at any size or color. Don't be afraid to experiment with the timing—it's really a personal preference. If you are dying for that first

taste of a sweet pepper, harvest it when it's small and still green. Then leave the next harvest on the vine longer, until it changes color, and see how you like it best. Although pepper plants can over-winter, the peppers themselves will not survive frost and should be harvested if frost threatens.

The nutritional content of a pepper is highest, and the pepper is the sweetest, when you leave it on the vine to reach its true color. For example, orange peppers are sweetest when they are orange, red peppers when they are red, etc. Picked at the peak of ripeness, the flavor of homegrown peppers is spectacular.

Pepper Storage and Eating Tips

To store peppers fresh, wrap them, unwashed, in a paper towel or dishcloth. Place them in a plastic bag and store in the refrigerator for 3 to 5 days.

To freeze, wash and dry your peppers. Pop in a freezer bag whole and place in freezer. Pull them out when you are ready to grill, stir-fry, or sauté. Freeze hot and sweet peppers in separate bags.

One of my favorite quick summertime meals is garden-fresh peppers, brushed with just a bit of olive oil, salt, and pepper, slightly blackened on the grill. Picked at the peak of ripeness, grilling or roasting sweet peppers caramelizes the sugars and brings out the sweetness. I like to grill up a huge batch, so we have them to eat all week long.

Pepper jelly is a super tasty way to preserve peppers. When made with a variety of peppers, it has a delightful combination of sweetness and spiciness and is stunning in small jelly jars. Pepper jelly is a huge crowd pleaser at a party poured over cream cheese and served with crackers. It also makes a lovely gift for any occasion.

For my video tutorial on how to make pepper jelly, please visit calikimgardenandhome.com/gardeningvideos.

How to Harvest a Pepper

Grasp the pepper in one hand and use scissors or pruners in the other hand to cut the pepper from the stem, close to the fruit. Don't pull them off the stem with your hands, as you could damage the plant.

CaliKim's Top Pepper Picks

California Wonder: Gorgeous, sweet red pepper; thick walled. Delicious on the grill or for stuffing.

Jimmy Nardello: Sweet Italian pepper; long, thin-skinned, ripens to a deep red. Delicious on the grill.

Cayenne Long Slim: Very hot, long thin pepper; ripens to a deep red color. Extremely productive. Adds a spicy hot zing to salsa or hot sauce.

Ancho: Mildly hot, thick walled, deep shiny green color. Extremely productive. Classic peppers for chile rellenos.

Cucumbers are one of the true joys of gardening. Every year, I look forward to celebrating summertime with this fresh-from-the-garden treat. Their crisp, crunch, light taste, and sweet flavor make them a delight to grow. I know you'll love them just as much as I do.

Cucumbers are ready to harvest and enjoy about 50 to 70 days from planting, depending on the variety you are growing and the weather conditions. Harvesting cucumbers when they are young is one of the secrets to sweet cucumbers. If they grow oversized, sometimes they'll taste bitter. The more often you harvest, the more the vines will produce and the longer they will produce. Once cucumbers start to appear on the vines, check daily because they grow quickly. Yellowing at the blossom end is a signal that the cucumber is overripe or is getting overheated in hot weather; pick immediately.

When to Harvest Cucumbers

For most varieties, the best size to harvest is when the cucumber is 6 to 10 inches (15 to 26 cm) in length. Check the directions on the seed packet for the best size for the variety you are growing. Experiment harvesting different varieties at different sizes to find the flavor you like best.

Cucumber Storage and Eating Tips

Wrap unwashed cucumbers in paper towels or a thin dishcloth. Put them in a plastic bag in the refrigerator. This absorbs excess moisture and helps them last longer. Stored this way, they will keep in the refrigerator for a week or so. Wash cukes when you are ready to use them. Washed and sliced cucumbers wrapped in paper towels will keep for 2 to 3 days.

Cucumbers have loads of crunch and flavor when picked fresh off the vine. We love to eat them as a refreshing snack, sliced and dipped in homemade hummus, in garden-fresh salads, or added to a sandwich for a light crunch. Their coolness is an ideal fresh side to a spicy main dish.

How to Harvest a Cucumber

Grasp the cucumber in one hand. Use scissors or pruners in the other hand to cut it from the vine, leaving about ¼ inch (6 mm) of the stem on the cucumber. Don't pull it off the vine as you could damage the plant.

CaliKim's Top Cucumber Picks

Spacemaster: Vining, disease resistant, 2- to 3-foot (60 to 90 cm) compact plant; container friendly. Produces cucumbers 6 to 10 inches (15 to 26 cm) long .

Marketmore: Vining, 4- to 5-foot (1.2- to 1.5-m) plant. Produces consistently until frost. Works well for canning or pickling.

Beit Alpha: Vining, 4- to 5-foot (1.2- to 1.5-m) plant, sweet slicing cuke, thin-skinned. Excellent for fresh eating, juicing, or salads.

HARVESTING SQUASH: POWER PRODUCER OF FOOD GALORE

If you are looking for a vegetable that is quick and simple to grow and produces fresh food galore, be sure to plant some squash in your garden. I love planting squash seeds. They germinate in just a few days and grow like wildfire—they're on my table in as little as 6 weeks.

Summer squash and winter squash are incredibly easy to grow, easy to harvest, and even more delicious to eat. See Chapter 7 for more details on each type.

When to Harvest Summer Squash

Summer squash, such as zucchini, crookneck, and pattypan squash, is ready to harvest 6 to 8 weeks from the time of planting, depending on the variety and weather conditions. Check your garden daily to see if the squash are ready. The more you pick, the more they will produce.

The secret to the best flavor for summer squash is to harvest when they are young and the skin and flesh are tender. Harvest zucchini or crookneck squash when they are 8 to 10 inches (20 to 26 cm) long. The gorgeous pattypan squash (also called scalloped) are ready when they are 3 to 4 inches (7.5 to 10 cm) in diameter.

Zucchini is famous for doubling in size within a day or two—watch out or you will end up with baseball bat–sized squash. Oversized summer squash skins tend to harden, and the flesh gets mealy and full of large seeds.

Summer Squash Storage and Eating Tips

Store summer squash unwashed, wrapped in a paper towel or thin dishcloth in a plastic bag in the refrigerator. It will keep for about 1 week.

Summer squash is a tasty addition to any summer breakfast, lunch, or dinner. It is super versatile and it can be prepared savory or sweet in a million and one ways. Some of my favorite ways to eat it are grilled, oven-roasted, stuffed, on homemade pizza, in omelets and quiches, or spiraled into "zoodles" with marinara sauce.

How to Harvest Summer Squash

Hold the squash in one hand close to the stem. Slowly and gently, so as not to damage the plant, twist the squash until the stem separates from the vine. An alternative method is to cut the stem carefully with a pair of pruners, leaving about 1 inch (2.5 cm) of the stem attached to the squash.

How to Harvest Winter Squash

The stems of ripe winter squash are very hard. Do not try to pull it from the vine, as you will damage the plant. Grasp the winter squash in one hand and cut it off the vine with a pair of sharp pruners in the other hand, leaving a few inches of stem attached to the squash. Short stems or no stems may cause bacteria to get into the squash where the stem was.

CaliKim's Top Squash Picks

SUMMER SQUASH

Early Prolific Straightneck Squash: Yellow, oblong, straight-necked bush variety.

Black Beauty Zucchini: Dark green, oblong bush variety.

Early White Scalloped (Pattypan): White, round, with scalloped edges, ornamental.

WINTER SQUASH

Butternut: Vining, tan peanut shape with orange, creamy flesh.

Spaghetti: Vining, bright yellow, very productive. Translucent strings shred easily with a fork once baked.

If you have picky non-veggie eaters in the house like I do, be a sneaky chef with summer squash. Peeled and shredded, it blends right in your favorite smoothie, muffin, cake, or spaghetti sauce recipes. Your picky eater will be none the wiser, and you'll feel great knowing that you are feeling your family healthy food (even if they don't know it).

Each summer, we grow a few baseball bat–sized zucchini. They are perfect for zucchini lasagna. Slice it and use it in place of noodles for a garden-fresh dinner that oozes with flavor. Once you try it, I know you will love it as much as our family does.

Whatever summer squash you can't eat fresh—and believe me, you'll have *a lot of it*—can be shredded and frozen for use in sauces, muffins, cakes, or cookies. Or slice it and freeze it on parchment paper–lined cookie sheets. Once

frozen, place slices in a freezer bag and store in the freezer for 2 to 3 months. There's nothing like pulling out garden-fresh squash from the freezer for some baked goods or zucchini lasagna when it's too cold to grow anything outside.

When to Harvest Winter Squash

Winter squash is ready to harvest 3 to 4 months from planting and should be left on the vine throughout the cooler days of fall and even into early winter. This helps the skin harden up so it will store through the winter. When ready for harvest, the classic varieties such as butternut squash will change from a light green to a solid tan; spaghetti squash will be bright yellow. No matter what variety of winter squash you are growing, the rind will be hard and difficult to pierce with your fingernail, and the stem will change from green to brown.

Winter Squash Storage and Eating Tips

Curing winter squash is a process that prepares it for storage. Simply let the squash sit at room temperature out of direct sunlight for a few weeks to harden the skin. Once the curing process is complete, store it in a cool (40–60°F/ 5–15°C), dry place. Don't let it freeze. Properly stored, it can last for 3 to 6 months.

Have some fun and use a few squash for fall table decorations.

You'll enjoy the fruit of your summer labors when you are eating delicious roasted winter squash in the dead of winter. Preparing it is a snap when it is baked whole before peeling and cutting, rather than trying to cut through the hard skin prior to baking. Once cooled, peel winter squash with a potato peeler and cube it. Or cut the squash in half and scoop out the flesh; use it mashed or as a base for marinara (spaghetti squash is delicious this way).

HARVESTING LETTUCE: FRESH, COLORFUL, AND CRISP

Imagine stepping outside to your backyard or patio to pick your own sweet, full-of-flavor lettuce. Nothing beats a crisp, colorful salad fresh from the garden; it's the classic garden meal. I love planting various types of lettuces in my garden. My salads look like a rainbow and have a variety of interesting textures.

When to Harvest Lettuce

Lettuce is ready to harvest 4 to 6 weeks from the time you plant seeds, depending on the weather. There is no hard-and-fast rule for what size lettuce leaves should be to harvest. It depends on the variety and your personal preference. Harvest the leaves when they are small for the sweet, tender baby leaves, or wait for larger, full-sized leaves. Pick in the morning for the sweetest flavor.

How to Harvest Lettuce

I like to use the "cut and come again" method when harvesting lettuce. Pinch off the outer leaves of the plant, leaving the center leaves to continue growing for later use. This will allow continual harvests from the same plant until it starts to form a center seed stalk (bolting). Bolting will change the flavor of the leaves, so you want to harvest before then. Harvest head lettuces by cutting off the head at the base of the plant.

CaliKim's Top Lettuce Picks

Prizehead: Loose-leaf type, large, ruffled, green maroon-tinged leaves. Heat tolerant.

Parris Island Cos: Romaine type, large upright green leaves. Heat tolerant.

Buttercrunch: Butterhead type, green, buttery, loose inner head. Slower to bolt.

Black Seeded Simpson: Loose-leaf type, bright green ruffled leaves. Heat tolerant.

Loose-leaf lettuce: Harvest when the leaves are 6 to 8 inches (15 to 20 cm) long.

Bibb or butterhead lettuce: Harvest when the inner leaves begin to form a loose head, or wait until they form a head 6 to 8 inches (15 to 20 cm) in diameter.

Romaine lettuce: Harvest when the leaves are elongated and overlap to form a fairly tight head about 6 to 8 inches (15 to 20 cm) tall.

Crisphead lettuce: Harvest when heads are firm and medium-sized, 6 to 8 inches (15 to 20 cm) in diameter.

Lettuce Storage and Eating Tips

Wash harvested lettuce in a sink full of water with a splash of white vinegar to kill any bugs that are lingering on the leaves. Rinse and lay out on a dish towel to dry, or dry in a salad spinner. Chop the lettuce into bite-sized piece, and place layers in a glass 9 × 13 inch (23 × 33 cm) dish between layers of paper towels. Place in the fridge. It will keep for about 5 days stored this way.

My favorite way to eat my fresh lettuce is a classic garden salad. For the past few years, we have developed a salad-a-day habit. This habit is easy to keep up on by prepping canning jar salads for the week. Chop your salad greens and other vegetables. In a mason jar, layer salad dressing and wet ingredients at the bottom of the jar: chopped tomatoes, carrots, peppers, and whatever other vegetables you like. Top the jar with your fresh salad greens. Meal prepping your salads gives you every reason to eat a healthy lunch—and no excuse not to.

For my video tutorial on how to harvest lettuce so it keeps on growing, please visit calikimgardenandhome.com/gardeningvideos.

HARVESTING PEAS: THE PERFECT GARDEN SNACK

Next to lettuce, peas are one of the easiest vegetables to grow. And they are certainly right up there with the tastiest of garden snacks. I love picking and eating them in the garden on a warm spring day. I'm sure you'll find—like I do—that your harvest basket of peas rarely makes it into the house.

There are three kinds of peas: garden peas, snap peas, and snow peas. Garden peas are shelled and eaten without a pod. Snap peas, also called sugar snap peas, are tender and very sweet, and they have edible pods. Snow peas have flat edible pods, and they are common in Asian cooking.

When to Harvest Peas

Most pea varieties are ready to harvest 6 to 8 weeks from the time you plant seeds. If you harvest too early, they may not have enough time to develop their sugars. Wait too long, and the pods will change to a yellow color and be tough and bitter. Temperatures over 75°F (23°C) can also make them tough and bitter.

How to Harvest Peas

Gently grasp the pea plant in one hand and the pea in another hand. Gently pull the pea from the stem. Don't pull the peas from the vine as you may damage the plant.

CaliKim's Top Pea Picks

Lincoln: Garden pea, prolific, compact vines, easy to shell, heat tolerant.

Sugar Ann: Snap pea, "All-America Selections" winner, very sweet, produces earlier than other sugar snap peas, compact vines.

Mammoth Melting: Snow pea, large pods, sweet tasting, 4-foot (1 m) plants.

For garden peas: Gently squeeze the pod when it looks fully plumped up. If you can feel the individual peas and there are no empty spaces, it is ready to harvest. Garden peas are the quickest maturing type.

For snap peas: Harvest when the peas plump out and fill out most of the pod.

For snow peas: Harvest when you can see through the pods when the sun shines through them, just as you see the small dots of peas beginning to form. Snow peas are the slowest maturing type.

Pea Storage and Eating Tips

Because of the high sugar content in peas, they are the most flavorful eaten fresh, before the sugar in the peas starts to break down.

Store any peas you don't eat right away unwashed and unshelled in the refrigerator in a glass dish between layers of paper towels to absorb excess moisture. They'll keep like this for 3 to 5 days.

Fresh peas can be blanched in boiling water for 1 to 2 minutes, placed in ice water to stop the cooking process, and then frozen for up to 6 months.

My favorite way to eat peas is fresh off the vine—dipped in hummus or as a salad topping—either in the pod (sugar snap or snow peas) or shelled (garden peas). Snow peas are delicious in a stir-fry with other homegrown veggies and with chicken, fish, or tofu.

SIMPLE HARVEST TIPS FOR OTHER POPULAR GARDEN VEGGIES

Beans: Cut or snap beans from the stem at pencil thickness, just when seeds start to bulge in the pod.

Beets: Gently pull beets from the soil when they are 2 to 3 inches (5 to 7.5 cm) in diameter. Place your finger in the soil to check for size. Leaves are edible.

Broccoli: Cut broccoli from the stem 2 to 3 inches (5 to 7.5 cm) below the heads when florets are dark green/blue and are tight and compact, before they open up. Leaves are edible. Side shoots may grow new heads.

Brussels Sprouts: Cut sprouts from stem from the bottom of the stem up when they are 1 inch in diameter. Do not pick leaves, as they are needed for growth of future sprouts.

Cabbage: Cut the head off at the base of the plant when leaves are crisp and form a tight head.

Carrots: Gently pull carrots from the soil when they are ½ to 1 inch (1 to 2.5 cm) in diameter. Place your finger in the soil to check for size. Tops are edible.

Cauliflower: Cut the head at the base when florets are firm, tight, and compact, before they open up and start to flower. White varieties should be white, purple varieties purple.

Celery: Cut stalks at the base of the plant when they are firm and glossy, 6 to 8 inches (15 to 20 cm) long. Leaves are edible.

Chard: For the sweetest flavor, pinch chard leaves off at the base of the stalk when they are the size of your palm or smaller. Stalks are edible.

Corn: To check an ear of corn, peel open a small section of the husk. It's ready to harvest when kernels are plump and a light, milky liquid oozes out when a kernel is pierced. Gently pull the ear of corn from the stalk. Remove husks just before eating.

Kale: Pinch from the stem when leaves are the size of your palm or smaller. Younger leaves will be more tender. Leaves will grow back in 2 to 3 weeks.

Lettuce: Cut head lettuce off at the base when leaves are crisp and form a tight head. For leaf lettuce, use the "cut and come again" method: Pinch off outer leaves at the base of the stem, leaving some inner leaves. Leaves grow back in 2 to 3 weeks.

Radishes: Gently pull from the soil when they are ½ to 1 inch (1 to 2.5 cm) in diameter. Place your finger in the soil to check for size. Tops are edible.

Spinach: Pinch leaves off at stem when they are the size of your palm or smaller. Small leaves will have the best flavor. Leaves will grow back in 2 to 3 weeks.

Now that you know a few simple tips for picking vegetables at the peak of ripeness and flavor, you'll feel confident showing off your own picture-perfect harvest baskets and sharing scrumptious, homegrown food with your loved ones. Harvesting and eating fresh, organic veggies that you grew yourself is worth every bit of effort you put into growing them, don't you think? You can now proudly say "I grew this" and revel in the many rewards of growing your own food.

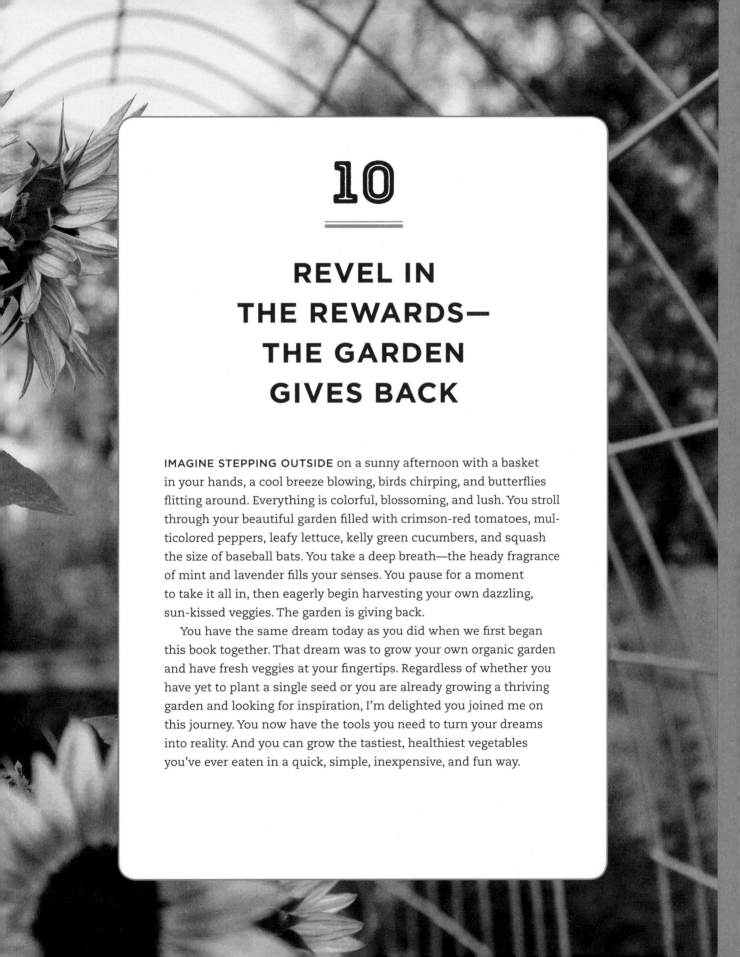

10

REVEL IN THE REWARDS— THE GARDEN GIVES BACK

IMAGINE STEPPING OUTSIDE on a sunny afternoon with a basket in your hands, a cool breeze blowing, birds chirping, and butterflies flitting around. Everything is colorful, blossoming, and lush. You stroll through your beautiful garden filled with crimson-red tomatoes, multicolored peppers, leafy lettuce, kelly green cucumbers, and squash the size of baseball bats. You take a deep breath—the heady fragrance of mint and lavender fills your senses. You pause for a moment to take it all in, then eagerly begin harvesting your own dazzling, sun-kissed veggies. The garden is giving back.

You have the same dream today as you did when we first began this book together. That dream was to grow your own organic garden and have fresh veggies at your fingertips. Regardless of whether you have yet to plant a single seed or you are already growing a thriving garden and looking for inspiration, I'm delighted you joined me on this journey. You now have the tools you need to turn your dreams into reality. And you can grow the tastiest, healthiest vegetables you've ever eaten in a quick, simple, inexpensive, and fun way.

You did it. You're a gardener now. I'm truly proud of you! You've taken steps to change your life and the lives of your loved ones by digging into what we've shared together on these pages. You worked hard; it's now time to revel in the rewards.

Getting your hands in the soil and feeling the warm sun on your back is pure joy. Planting seeds and nurturing your garden. Harvesting your own sun-ripened food, free from synthetic chemicals.

But the rewards don't stop there. The payoff reaches far beyond growing and harvesting your own organic vegetables.

THE REWARD: GARDENING COMMUNITY

One of the greatest pleasures of growing your own food is gardening in community with like-minded people. We're all here to support and lift each other up through the highs and lows of growing veggies. This can be as informal as a chat with a neighbor or friend about what they're

growing or talking to other gardeners who live near you to find out what grows best in your area. It might mean that you rent a plot at a community garden or join a local garden club. There are plenty of online groups that are a wealth of support and knowledge. Join a Facebook gardening group or watch YouTube videos and join in the discussion in the comments. We're all in this together, and no one needs to be alone in their gardening journey.

THE REWARD: SHARING

When I first started gardening, my dream was simple. I wanted to grow enough fresh veggies for my family so that I didn't have to buy produce at the grocery store. That was it. I had no idea where this dream would take me. At the time, I had no desire to start a YouTube channel or make gardening videos. The thought that my full-time career would someday be teaching thousands of people from all over the world how to grow organic vegetables was the furthest thing from my mind. Growing organic vegetables has changed my life, the lives of my family, and the lives of people all over the world.

How did this happen? I discovered early on one of the most rewarding fruits of my labor comes from sharing. Coworkers, extended family, friends, and neighbors love the zucchini, eggplant, and homegrown tomatoes we share with them—and this is hugely satisfying. Equally fulfilling for me is the ability to share what I am truly passionate about: teaching people how to grow their own food and leading them to experience the joy and garden magic for themselves. The more I shared, the more the garden gave back—in more ways than I ever imagined.

I met my dear friend Kristy through the YouTube garden community. Kristy has a chronic neurological condition with debilitating pain. The pain gave her few options other than to lie in bed. She had to give up her job as a nurse. She was depressed and her nutrition was poor. She would stare out the window and think "someday I'll grow my own veggies and get healthy again." One day, she searched "gardening" on YouTube and our channel came up in the search results. She watched a few videos and realized that growing veggies wasn't as difficult as she thought. She quickly fell in love with gardening and it became her therapy. Growing her own organic vegetables helped her realize she was able to use food as medicine to nourish her body and help restore a new passion for life. Her outlook completely turned around, as did her nutrition and health. She eventually became certified as a Master Gardener, and she now shares her love of growing organic vegetables with others. The garden is giving back.

Patricia, a longtime YouTube viewer, made this comment on a video: "I live in a small town with only one grocery store. Their produce is not good. I am so glad I learned how to grow my own vegetables from you, Kim. I need it now more than ever. I was diagnosed with rheumatoid arthritis 10 years ago and was in remission for many years. My doctor says I am now slipping out of remission and need to follow an anti-inflammatory diet, with lots of organic veggies and fruits. He gave me 6 months to get it under control or we start drug trials again. I am learning from you how to grow my own organic produce and hopefully I won't have to rely on medication."

I don't know who is blessed more—Kristy and Patricia, or me. We all share in the joy. The garden is giving back—all three of us are reaping the rewards of what we have sown.

While you may or may not start a YouTube channel or have a career teaching organic gardening, you can share what you love to do. Give a packet of seeds to a neighbor. Make homemade salsa for a friend. Teach your kids how to grow lettuce. Share your love of gardening in one small way with one single person. You never know how it will bring a smile to a child's face, change a friend's health, make a difference in someone's day, or even change their life. You will be as blessed as they are.

You can grow your own organic garden grocery store and bring that basket, brimming with freshness and flavor, in your kitchen to prepare a garden-fresh meal of nourishing, delicious food for your family.

Turn your dreams into reality. Revel in the rewards that growing an organic garden has to offer. Start simple by planting just one seed. Expand your garden as your skills and confidence grow. You never know where it will take you.

Don't delay. Your garden is waiting for you.

Appendix 1
CALIKIM'S QUICK LOOK— WARM-WEATHER VEGGIES

Tomatoes

How to Start → from seed indoors, transplants

Best Time to Plant Outdoors → late spring, early summer, early fall in temperate climates

Sun → full sun, 6 to 12 hours/day

Soil Planting Temperature → at least 60°F (15°C)

Best Growing Temperature → 60–90°F (15–32°C)

Germination Temperature → 60–85°F (15–30°C)

Germination Time → 5 to 10 days

Plant Height → 3–8 feet (1–3 m)

Plant Spacing → 2–3 feet (60–90 cm)

Seed to Table → 45 to 90 days

Tomato Tips → Support with a cage or trellis.

Peppers

How to Start → from seed indoors, transplants

Best Time to Plant Outdoors → late spring, early summer

Sun → full sun, 8 to 10 hours per day

Soil Planting Temperature → at least 60°F (15°C)

Best Growing Temperature → 60–90°F (15–32°C)

Germination Temperature → 70–85°F (15–30°C)

Germination Time → 7 to 21 days

Plant Height → 1–2 feet (30–60 cm)

Plant Spacing → 1–2 feet (30–60 cm)

Seed to Table → 60 to 100 days

Pepper Tips → Use a heat mat to start seeds indoors. Support with a small tomato cage. Prune and mulch to overwinter.

WARM-WEATHER VEGGIES

Cucumbers

How to Start ➜ from seed indoors, direct seed, transplants

Best Time to Plant Outdoors ➜ late spring, early summer

Sun ➜ full sun, 6 to 8 hours per day

Soil Planting Temperature ➜ at least 60°F (15°C)

Best Growing Temperature ➜ 65–90°F (15–32°C)

Germination Temperature ➜ 60–85°F (15–30°C)

Germination Time ➜ 3 to 7 days

Plant Height ➜ 2–6 feet (60–180 cm)

Plant Spacing ➜ 1–2 feet (30–60 cm)

Seed to Table ➜ 6 to 8 weeks

Cucumber Tips ➜ Support with a trellis. Provide afternoon shade in hot climates.

Squash

How to Start ➜ from seed indoors, direct seed, transplants

Best Time to Plant Outdoors ➜ late spring, early summer, late summer

Sun ➜ full sun, 6 to 10 hours per day

Soil Planting Temperature ➜ at least 60°F (15°C)

Best Growing Temperature ➜ 65–90°F (15–32°C)

Germination Temperature ➜ 60–85°F (15–30°C)

Germination Time ➜ 2 to 7 days

Plant Height ➜ 2–8 feet (60–240 cm)

Plant Spacing ➜ 2–4 feet (60–120 cm)

Seed to Table ➜ 50 to 120 days

Squash Tips ➜ Grow vining types on a trellis. Check daily for harvest once fruit sets.

Appendix 2

CALIKIM'S QUICK LOOK— COOL-WEATHER VEGGIES

Lettuce

How to Start → from seed indoors, direct seed, transplants

Best Time to Plant Outdoors → early spring, early summer, fall, winter in temperate climates

Sun → full sun (6+ hours) in temps under 75°F (23°C), part shade in hotter temps

Soil Planting Temperature → 35–75°F (10–23°C) (highest germination rate at 75°F)

Best Growing Temperature → 40–75°F (5–23°C)

Germination Temperature → 50–75°F (10–23°C)

Germination Time → 2 to 7 days

Plant Height → 6–12 inches (15–30 cm)

Plant Spacing → 2–6 inches (5–15 cm)

Seed to Table → 4 to 6 weeks

Lettuce Tips → Lettuce will survive light frosts. Plant seeds every 2 weeks to keep the harvest coming. Shade in warm weather. Container friendly.

Peas

How to Start → from seed indoors, direct seed transplants

Best Time to Plant Outdoors → early spring, early summer, fall, winter in temperate climates

Sun → full sun (6+ hours) in temps under 75°F (23°C), part sun (4 hours) in hotter temps

Soil Planting Temperature → 40–75°F (10–23°C) (highest germination rate at 75°F)

Best Growing Temperature → 40–75°F (10–23°C)

Germination Temperature → 50–75°F (10–23°C)

Germination Time → 2 to 7 days

Plant Height → 2–8 feet (½–2 m)

Plant Spacing → 1–2 feet (30–60 cm)

Seed to Table → 6 to 10 weeks

Pea Tips → Grow vining types on a trellis. Shade in hot weather. Container friendly. Great to plant with kids.

GLOSSARY

Basic Gardening Terms Explained

Bolting: Many greens and cool-weather vegetables shoot up a tall stalk from the center of the plant in temperatures over 80°F (27°C). Flowers will form on this center stalk. When the flowers dry, seeds can be harvested. This is nature's way of producing the next generation of plants.

Compost: A decayed mixture of organic material that is used to fertilize your garden plants. A compost pile can be made by gathering fruit and veggie scraps, grass clippings, leaves, and other organic material into a pile and letting it rot. Referred to by gardeners as "black gold."

Cool-Weather Vegetables: Vegetables that grow best in daytime temperatures between 40°F (5°C) to 75°F (23°C). Many cool-weather veggies will even tolerate light frosts (32°F/0°C), especially if the plants are well established when frost hits.

Cotyledon (baby leaves): When a seed germinates, this is the first set of leaves that appears. They are part of the embryonic plant. They will fall off or can be pinched off as the "true leaves" appear and take over the job of feeding the plant.

Determinate Tomatoes: A compact 2- to 4-foot (60- to 120-cm) tomato type that grows to a set height. The tomatoes ripen all at once, usually within 2 to 3 weeks, then the plant dies.

Direct Seed: The process of planting seeds directly into soil outside, rather than starting them indoors and then transplanting them later outside.

Frost Date: The average date when the first frost of the fall or winter season occurs, or the last date frost occurs in the winter/early spring. These dates are important because they determine when you can plant crops that are not frost tolerant. Date varies by location.

Germinate: When a seed sprouts and breaks out of the seed shell.

Hardening Off: The transition process of acclimating plants growing indoors to growing outdoors. This process should be done gradually so the seedlings become hardier; when they are slowly introduced to the outdoor elements, plants are better able to survive full outdoor exposure.

Indeterminate Tomatoes: A type of tomato that grows vines 6 to 10 feet (1.8 to 3 m). They grow and produce tomatoes throughout the growing season until frost kills the plant. They grow best with a cage or sturdy trellis to support the plant.

Leggy: A seedling with thin, long stems, usually caused by inadequate light or by growing too far from an overhead light source.

Microbes: Microscopic organisms that can't be seen with the naked eye. In garden soil, they digest organic matter and improve the structure of the soil.

Mulch: A material such as wood chips, leaves, or straw that is placed around plants, or over the soil. Mulch helps soil retain moisture, regulates soil temperature, improves soil fertility, suppresses weeds, and helps prevent erosion.

Organic Garden: A garden that is grown with natural methods using compost, organic soils and fertilizers, and natural methods of pest and disease control, without using synthetic fertilizers or pesticides.

Pollination: The transfer of pollen from the male part of a flower to the female part of a flower so that the plant can produce seeds.

Powdery Mildew: A common fungal disease that can affect a wide range of plants, typically squash, cucumbers, beans, peas, and some flowers. It starts as white fuzzy spots on the leaves and it can rapidly spread to the entire leaf and entire plant. It can weaken and, if severe, kill the plant.

Rootbound: When a plant outgrows its container and the roots begin wrapping around inside the bottom of the container. Once a plant becomes rootbound, it's usually not getting the nutrients it needs and often becomes stunted.

Set Fruit: When a plant starts growing fruit on it. Most of the vegetables we eat are botanically classified as fruits, including tomatoes, peppers, cucumbers, and squash. If there are seeds inside your veggie, it's actually a fruit. Similar terms are "fruit set" or "setting fruit."

True Leaves (adult leaves): The set of leaves that form as a seedling grows. They look more like what the plant's leaves will look like when mature. The true leaves feed the plant as it grows as the cotyledons (baby leaves) drop off. Many plants can be transplanted when two sets of true leaves develop.

Warm-Weather Vegetables: Veggies that thrive when planted in warm soil (at least 50–60°F/10–16°C) when the nighttime temperatures are 60–75°F (15–23°C) and daytime temperatures are 75–90°F (23–32°C). Cool temperatures (less than 60°F/15°C) or overly hot temperatures (over 90°F/32°C) slow their growth. Warm-weather veggies are cold sensitive, and frost will kill the plant in most cases.

RESOURCES

SEEDS

CaliKim Garden & Home:
calikimgardenandhome.com

CONTAINERS

Smart Pots
smartpots.com
Fabric containers, fabric raised beds

SOIL AND FERTILIZER

Good Dirt
good-dirt.com
Indoor and outdoor potting mix, soil conditioner
(for garden beds), plant food

VermisTerra
vermisterra.com
Worm castings, worm tea

Visit calikimgardenandhome.com for discount
codes on the above products.

OTHER GARDEN SUPPLIES

Visit calikimgardenandhome.com/
gardensupplies for links to the following.
Alternatively, you can look for these items
online or at your favorite garden center.

GROW LIGHTS

Clamp Light Setup
8.5-inch Clamp Light
LED bulb
CFL bulb

Shop Light Setup
Shop Light Fixture, 4-foot (122 cm) (bulb not
    included)
Fluorescent lightbulbs, 4-foot (122 cm)
Shop Light Fixture, 2-foot (60 cm) (bulb included)
LED shop light fixture, 4-foot (122 cm)
    (bulb included)

Tabletop Light Setup

Timers
Power strip with timer
Timer (electrical outlet)

SEED-STARTING SUPPLIES

Peat Pellets
Large (3 inches, 50 mm)
Small (1 inch, 36 mm)

Seed-Starting 3" (50 mm) Pots

Seedling Heat Mat

Seed-Starting Cells

Plant Labels

Plant Trays

WATERING

Drip Irrigation Kit

Screen Filter (Hose Thread)

Drip Irrigation Timer (Programmable,
Two Outlet, Hose Thread)

Moisture Meter

PEST AND DISEASE CONTROL

Neem Oil

Natural Soap

MISCELLANEOUS GARDEN SUPPLIES

Shade Cloth

Pruners

ABOUT THE AUTHOR

CaliKim lives in Southern California with her husband, Jerry; her two children, Julianne and Drew; and their border collie, Mac. She is an urban gardener who is passionate about growing organic vegetables. She believes growing your own healthy, delicious food doesn't have to be complicated, take a lot of time, or cost a lot of money. She provides step-by-step instructions on how to grow an organic vegetable garden in a quick, simple, and inexpensive way.

Kim and Jerry (aka "CameraGuy"), love being outside together and work as a team to produce garden content in video, still photography, and written form. Their YouTube channel, CaliKim Garden & Home DIY, has an extensive library of garden video tutorials, with millions of views from gardeners worldwide. Kim provides garden support and shares garden how-tos, tips, and healthy garden-to-table recipes through their YouTube channel, blog, online seed shop, and social media communities.

WHERE TO FIND CALIKIM

Seed and Garden Shop: calikimgardenandhome.com
Garden Blog: calikimgardenandhome.com/category/blog
YouTube: youtube.com/user/CaliKim29

Instagram: instagram.com/calikim29
Facebook: facebook.com/CaliKimGardenandHomeDIY
Email: calikim@calikimgardenandhome.com

INDEX

A

air pruning, 76, 105
Amish Paste tomato, 131
Ancho pepper, 133

B

backup plants, 125
barriers, 119
beans, 143
beds
    in-ground garden beds, 70–71
    raised garden beds, 72–75
beets, 143
Beit Alpha cucumber, 135
bibb lettuce, 140
Black Beauty zucchini, 138
Black Seeded Simpson lettuce, 140
bolting, 23
bottom watering, 52
broccoli, 143
Brussels sprouts, 143
Buttercrunch lettuce, 140
butterhead lettuce, 140
Butternut squash, 138

C

cabbage, 143
California Wonder pepper, 133
carrots, 143
cauliflower, 143
Cayenne Long Slim pepper, 133
celery, 143
chard, 143
clamp lights, 41–42
cold-weather protection, 125
community, 146
companion plants, 119
compost, 69
container gardens, 76–77
cool-weather vegetables
    basics, 23
    cucumbers, 100–104
    lettuce, 111–112
    peas, 113–114
    planting, 23
    sunlight, 110
    timing, 110
corn, 143
crisphead lettuce, 140
cucumbers
    Beit Alpha, 135
    cages for, 102
    eating tips, 135
    germination, 150

    harvesting, 135
    Marketmore, 135
    planting seedlings, 101
    planting seeds, 102
    Quick Look, 150
    seeds, 100–101, 102
    shade, 100
    Spacemaster, 135
    spacing, 102
    storage tips, 135
    stress and, 100
    support, 102–104
    teepee trellis, 104

D

determinate tomatoes, 130
diseases
    backup plants, 125
    milk spray, 123
    prevention, 118–119
    pruning and, 123
drip irrigation
    automating, 89
    benefits, 85
    disease reduction and, 85
    efficiency of, 85
    frequency determination, 89
    installation, 68, 85, 86–88
    introduction, 83
    roots and, 85
    timer, 89
    time savings with, 85
    versatility of, 85

E

Early Prolific Straightneck squash, 138
Early White Scalloped (Pattypan) squash, 138

F

fertilizer
    organic food and, 16
    organic seed and, 32
    seedlings and, 53
    warm-weather vegetables, 93
frost dates, 25, 27

G

garden peas, 142
germination
    cucumbers, 150
    lettuce, 151
    peas, 151
    peppers, 97, 149

squash, 150
    tomatoes, 94, 149
grow light box, 43–44

H
"hardening off," 61–63
harvest
    beans, 143
    beets, 143
    broccoli, 143
    Brussels sprouts, 143
    cabbage, 143
    carrots, 143
    cauliflower, 143
    celery, 143
    chard, 143
    continuing, 129
    corn, 143
    cucumbers, 135
    experimenting with, 129
    kale, 143
    lettuce, 139–140, 143
    peas, 114, 141–142, 143
    peppers, 132–133
    radishes, 143
    rules for, 128
    spinach, 143
    squash, 137–138
    summer squash, 137
    tomatoes, 130–131
    winter squash, 137, 138
hot-weather protection, 125

I
indeterminate tomatoes, 130
indoor grow lights
    amount of, 49
    automating, 50
    clamp lights, 41–42
    clamp light station, 42
    distance to seedling, 49
    grow light box, 43–44
    introduction, 39
    kelvin, 40
    lumens, 39–40
    mistakes to avoid, 49–50
    shop light setup, 45–46
    shop light station, 47
    tabletop grow light, 48
in-ground garden beds, 70–71
irrigation, 68, 83–89

J
Jimmy Nardello pepper, 133

K
kale, 143
Kellogg's Breakfast tomato, 131
kelvin, 40

L
lettuce
    bibb, 140
    Black Seeded Simpson, 140
    bolting, 23
    Buttercrunch, 140
    butterhead, 140
    crisphead, 140
    eating tips, 140
    germination, 151
    growing in containers, 112
    harvesting, 139–140, 143
    loose-leaf, 140
    Parris Island Cos, 140
    planting, 111–112
    Prizehead, 140
    Quick Look, 151
    romaine, 140
    storage tips, 140
light. See indoor grow lights; sunlight.
Lincoln pea, 142
location. See placement.
loose-leaf lettuce, 140

M
Mammoth Melting pea, 142
Marketmore cucumber, 135
milk spray, 123
mulch, 82

N
Neem oil, 121–122
non-organic seeds, 32

O
organic seeds, 32
overwintering, 99

P
Parris Island Cos lettuce, 140
peas
    fall crop, 114
    garden peas, 142
    germination, 151
    harvesting, 114, 141–142
    Lincoln, 142
    Mammoth Melting, 142
    pea, 143
    planting, 113–114
    Quick Look, 151
    seeds, 113–114
    snap peas, 142
    snow peas, 142
    spacing, 114
    spring crop, 114
    Sugar Ann, 142
    support, 114

peat pellets
    starting seeds in, 34–35
    transplanting into larger containers, 59
    watering, 34, 52
peppermint oil, 122
peppers
    Ancho, 133
    California Wonder, 133
    Cayenne Long Slim, 133
    eating tips, 133
    germination, 97, 149
    harvesting, 132–133
    Jimmy Nardello, 133
    overwintering, 99
    planting, 97–98
    Quick Look, 149
    seeds, 97
    storage tips, 133
pests
    backup plants, 125
    barriers, 119
    companion plants, 119
    Neem Oil, 121–122
    peppermint oil, 122
    prevention, 118–119, 120–123
    soap and water, 121
    water and, 120
placement
    distance to home, 66
    sun exposure, 66–67
    water source, 68
planting
    cool-weather vegetables, 110
    cucumbers, 101, 102
    lettuce, 111–112
    peas, 113–114
    peppers, 97–98
    squash, 107, 108
    tomatoes, 94–95
    warm-weather vegetables, 92–93
Prizehead lettuce, 140
projects
    clamp light setup, 41–42
    clamp light station, 42
    container gardens, 77
    cucumber cages, 102
    drip irrigation installation, 86–88
    grow light box, 43–44
    in-ground garden beds, 71
    portable shop light station, 47
    raised garden beds, 74–75
    shop light setup, 45–46
    starting seeds in peat pellets, 33–35
    starting seeds in soil, 36–38
    tabletop grow light, 48
    tomato cages, 96
pruning
    air pruning, 76, 105
    diseases and, 123
    tomatoes, 94

Q
Quick Look
    cucumbers, 150
    lettuce, 151
    peas, 151
    peppers, 149
    squash, 150
    tomatoes, 149

R
radishes, 143
raised garden beds, 72–75
romaine lettuce, 140

S
seedlings
    distance to indoor grow lights, 49
    fertilizing, 53
    "hardening off," 61–63
    non-organic seeds, 32
    organic seeds, 32
    purchasing, 109
    selecting, 31–32
    sourcing, 32
    starting in peat pellets, 33–35
    starting in pots with soil, 36–38
    transplanting into larger containers, 58–60
    transplanting into outdoor gardens, 61–63
    watering, 51–52
seeds
    cucumber, 100–101, 102
    lettuce, 111–112
    peas, 113–114
    peppers, 97
    squash, 108
    tomato, 94
sharing, 146–147
shop lights, 45–46
shop light station, 47
snap peas, 142
snow peas, 142
soil
    bagged soil, 69
    compost, 69
    disease prevention and, 118–119
    health of, 118–119
    pest prevention and, 118–119
    temperature of, 93
Spacemaster cucumber, 135
spacing
    for cucumbers, 102
    peas, 114
    squash, 108–109
    tomatoes, 95
Spaghetti squash, 138
spinach, 143
sprays, 121–123
squash
    Black Beauty zucchini, 138

Butternut, 138
Early Prolific Straightneck, 138
Early White Scalloped (Pattypan), 138
eating tips, 137–138
germination, 150
harvesting, 137–138
planting seedlings, 107
planting seeds, 108
Quick Look, 150
seeds, 108
spacing for bush variety, 109
spacing for vine varieties, 108
Spaghetti, 138
storage tips, 137
summer squash, 106, 137
transplant sourcing, 109
types of, 106
winter squash, 106
staking, 96
storage
cucumbers, 135
lettuce, 140
peppers, 133
squash, 137, 138
summer squash, 137
tomatoes, 131
winter squash, 138
Sugar Ann pea, 142
summer squash
Black Beauty Zucchini, 138
Early Prolific Straightneck Squash, 138
Early White Scalloped (Pattypan) squash, 138
eating tips, 137–138
harvesting, 106, 137
storage tips, 137
sunlight
cool-weather vegetables, 110
placement considerations, 66–67
warm-weather vegetables, 93
support
for cucumbers, 102–104
for peas, 114
for peppers, 98–99
for tomatoes, 96

T
tabletop grow light, 48
teepee trellis, 104
Tiny Tim tomato, 131
tomatoes
Amish Paste, 131
cages for, 96
determinate, 130
eating tips, 131
germination, 94, 149
harvesting, 130–131
indeterminate, 130
Kellogg's Breakfast, 131
planting, 94–95
pruning, 94

Quick Look, 149
seeds, 94
spacing, 95
staking, 96
storage tips, 131
support for, 96
Tiny Tim, 131
transplanting, 60
Yellow Brandywine, 131
transplanting
"hardening off," 61–63
into larger containers, 58–60
introduction, 56
timing, 56–57
tomatoes, 60
to outdoor garden, 61–63

W
warm-weather vegetables
basics, 24
fertilizer, 93
frost dates, 24–25, 27
peppers, 97–99
planting, 92–93
soil temperature, 93
squash, 105–109
sunlight, 93
timing, 92–93
tomatoes, 94–96
water, 93
water
amount, 80
bottom watering, 52
drip irrigation, 68, 83–89
frequency, 81
irrigation, 68, 83–89
location, 80
peat pellets, 52
pest prevention with, 120
placement and, 68
seedlings and, 51–52
technique, 81
timing, 80
warm-weather vegetables, 93
weather challenges, 125
weeds, 120
winter squash
Butternut squash, 138
eating tips, 138
harvesting, 106, 137, 138
Spaghetti squash, 138
storage tips, 138

Y
Yellow Brandywine tomato, 131
YouTube, 14–15

Z
zucchini, 138